CRUMMY
CONVERSATIONS

FOREWORD BY DR. VANESSA LAPOINTE

HOW TO TALK WITH KIDS ABOUT DEATH, DIVORCE, DIAGNOSIS, DISASTER AND DEPARTURE

Published in Canada, for Global Distribution by YGTMedia Co.
www.ygtmedia.co/publishing
To order additional copies of this book:
publishing@ygtmedia.co

Edited by Christine Stock
Cover & book design by Doris Chung
ePub & Kindle Editions by Ellie Sipilä

Author Photo by Ashley Marston Photography

CRUMMY
CONVERSATIONS

FOREWORD BY DR. VANESSA LAPOINTE

HOW TO TALK WITH KIDS ABOUT DEATH, DIVORCE, DIAGNOSIS, DISASTER AND DEPARTURE

MICHELLE A. SURTEES, M.ED

To all life's uncomfortable and painful changes. A love note.

TABLE OF CONTENTS

FOREWORD

As a registered psychologist and parent educator with more than twenty years' experience, I want to share with you the number one question I get asked. It goes like this: "What do I DO when . . ." The truth is, I don't have an answer. And I believe if we are really going to show up in the best possible way for our children, we need to stay firm in the understanding that it is not about knowing *what to do.*

Rather, as it turns out, we've been asking the wrong question all along. Perhaps the question is: "How should I BE when . . ." Why? Because the DOING flows from the BEING. How you are on the inside, what you embody energetically, the essence of how you show up in that moment—all of this is going to create a certain kind of DOING. And I can dole out scripts of what to say and lists of what to do to those who seek my counsel. But if the doing is not infused with a being-ness that is full of swagger and heart, then all of it will go sideways—for you and for your child.

And this right here is the gift of the book you are holding in your hands. Michelle Surtees has very capably put into words what it is to BE for your child so that you can manifest a DOING kind response that will have hope, adaptation, resilience, and growth alive for you both. Surtees breathes life into the concept of swagger as she capably guides parents and other big people into a philosophy that will allow them to show up for their children in ways that really matter as they navigate the inevitable storms of life.

Surtees has cleverly offered a "recipe" that is the anti-script I have always wished I could direct parents to when they are so desperately seeking answers for how to have the most challenging of conversations with their children. Her research-based and heart-centered approach takes into account the being of the adult, the heart of the child, and the reality of how hard it can be to confidently step off into the abyss of big conversations about significant, messy, and difficult topics.

This book offers a lifeline. As Surtees so eloquently captures, navigating life's difficult conversations and experiences isn't about making it all better. Rather, it is about having the child really feel cared for and understood. You don't need to know the answers; you get to BE the answer. With her well-thought-out approach, Surtees will guide you to exactly the place and space you need to be in order to show up as exactly this.

So, pour yourself a big cup of tea and get ready to enjoy some delicious cookies. Life can be hard. Very, very hard. There is no taking the sting out of that reality. But where there is challenge, there is opportunity for growth. As someone who has witnessed children and their grown-ups come through horrible life events and not just survive them but actually thrive, I, along with Surtees, am here to tell you there really is hope on the horizon. And just like that delectable cookie, let me tell you *how sweet it is.* Dive into Surtees's book, follow her recipe, and trust. It can and will be okay.

DR. VANESSA LAPOINTE

REGISTERED PSYCHOLOGIST, PARENTING EDUCATOR, AND MOM

A NOTE ABOUT THIS BOOK'S STRUCTURE

This book uses chocolate chip cookies as a metaphor, and I can't think of a better way to offer you this communication method. I also can't think of a better way to talk about connection, relationship, presence, and love with and for a child than to frame it all in the context of a warm, gooey-centered, crispy-edged, perfectly baked chocolate chip cookie.

Crummy Conversations has two main sections. Section One (Chapters 1–7) talks about the current problem, discusses the solution, and offers ideas about why this matters, who this is for, what change we are talking about, where we can implement the solution, and how it can be used. Basically, it's the *who, what, where,* and *how* of this book.

In Section Two (Chapters 8–13), we look at the solution in detail. These chapters review the Courage to Communicate Model by considering it in three parts. These chapters share the experience someone else has had with change while also offering you questions to consider your own experience. The stories you will read were shared with me without the individuals having knowledge of this book's content. I simply asked individuals in my life to share a story about change, and what you will read are unaltered versions of what was shared with me.

A BETTER BATTER

I was recently browsing through a major bookstore, one that tends to be referred to as the giant of all brick-and-mortar bookstores. You know that one that is named after the sections in books? That one. With a latte in hand, my eyes were trying to look past the flashy covers on display, the over-priced yet luxurious-looking blankets and pillows, and the factory-made yet totally adorable mugs and totes with the hope of finding the Parenting section. I thought I had located it, but it appeared to be all pregnancy and baby books, so I lapped around to the other side of the shelf, only to find myself surrounded by thesauri and dictionaries. Lap number three confirmed that this tiny section was, in fact, everything that was available in this store under the parenting genre category. So, I dug through some titles, looking for something compelling that called to me. Literally on my knees and squinting at the bottom shelf, I found one or two titles that could be considered classics, but nothing that screamed *buy me! I will inspire and motivate you to reach your* *full potential as a tired mother of three fueled by caffeine and good intentions.* Dejected, I left the section and found myself wandering over to the adult Self-Help section. Now THIS is a section. Full of evocative titles and glossy hardcovers, this section is robust. Here, you can find a book that pretty much addresses any genre of self-help that interests you. There are rows and rows of memoirs surrounded by gorgeous covers that will assist you in finding JOY in the Tuscan countryside, happiness in your organized home, faith in your kitchen, and romance in your bedroom. If I stayed in this section long enough, I could learn to launch my own career in any occupation I want, repair my body from years of neglect, retrain my mind to think positively, and literally, unf*ck myself. Pushing further into the section, I came upon the back wall, the epicenter of the Self-Help section: the "how to heal thyself" section. This section offered me an approach to heal from anything and everything that's ever happened to me. If someone wants to deal with some dark and scary shenanigans that happened many years ago, they can find the book here. As I stood looking up the wall, I thought two things: 1) the self-help industry must be a billion-dollar industry, and 2) imagine if the Parenting section had this much money invested in it?

Adults are spending thousands of dollars trying to figure out how to heal from the past and thrive in the future, and it's not just in book purchases. The online world is full of masterclasses and coaching courses and strategies and tools that, if implemented, can change everyday lives. The money people invest in this industry is a testament to their dedication for growth and expansion as a global community and as individuals. It's a hope story of sorts. It is also an example of the deep and damaging hurt that many people carry with them. It seems people continue to spend more money and effort on dealing with the results of their emotional problems instead of trying to prevent them.[1] It also seems to be the case that childhood life experiences didn't have to be tragic for someone to feel that their emotional needs weren't met as children and that the consequences of that lack of attunement to their needs can do lasting damage. I have to wonder whether the Self-Help section would take up as much floor space if we invested a few more beautiful covers and catchy titles in the Parenting section. If we invested more into supporting and resourcing adults who were raising children, would we have fewer adults spending the latter part of their lives trying to understand what happened in their own childhoods? Imagine if we gave children the skills in childhood most of us are trying to learn in adulthood? Imagine if Children's Wellness was the most invested-in genre in every bookstore? Imagine if we made a global investment in the prevention of childhood trauma instead of an investment in the intervention of adult mental health?

The twist on this Self-Help versus Parenting section observation is that some of us are, for the most part, a group of adults doing our own emotional and therapeutic work to benefit our children. As caring adults, we know we need to do this work to benefit the next generation. As human beings, we know that in times of stress or perceived danger, we seek connection and safety in other people,[2] and so we find ourselves searching for our people, and we watch our children searching for us. The same instinct that drives our children to seek out our comfort when they cry is the same instinct that draws us to the world of self-help and therapy. Our deep desire for connection is a basic primal instinct that our subconscious mind looks for instinctively,[3] and that need for connection is why we so desperately want to be there for our children, physically and emotionally. When the world swirls around a tragedy or a trauma, we have a primal need as humans to connect to each other. Our cells tell us to seek support from those around us and to offer support to others. We want to be surrounded by people who know us, love us, and understand us. Our brains want to understand what has happened and what might happen next to make it less scary, and our hearts and souls want to know we are not alone in our confusion, fear, and grief. When things get hard, we desperately want community, connection, and leadership. We flounder without support. We need support in the form of connection for ourselves, and we want to be that support and connection for our children.

But we don't always know how.

We see the statistics about how our children's unmet emotional needs are impacting their lives, and we know that 20 percent[4] of Canadian youth have a mental health disorder and that one in eleven children and youth are pre-scribed medication to stabilize mood, anxiety, or depression. In the last two years, the number of children with anxiety and depression has doubled. Research is now reporting that a staggering one in five children is affected by anxiety and one in four[5] is impacted by depression. The statistics can be scary. Who wants to focus on the fact that depression is the leading cause of disability worldwide and that by 2030, necessary worldwide mental health supports[6] could cost the global economy up to $16 trillion? I also could have lived without knowing that "close to 800,000 people die due to suicide every year (one person every 40 seconds)" and suicide "is the second leading cause of death among 15–29-year-olds."[7] We intellectually understand that the chal-lenges our children experience in their daily lives contribute to the reason why 57 percent of youth report using alcohol and that 20 percent[8] report using street drugs. We do not want our children to become one of the 30 percent[9] of girls in Canada showing signs of eating disorders or one of the 31,003[10] children and youth who were reported as runaways in 2018. And the United

States reports 460,000[11] runaways a year and confirms that 91 percent of those children are considered endangered. Plus, there are so many risks related to the internet that were never a part of the realm of consideration just a decade or two ago. In the last five years, the risk of online child luring has increased by 37 percent and the incidents of non-consensual distribution of intimate images increased by a horrendous 80 percent.[12] We know our children need us, and we want to talk to them about the hard things. We truly want to listen to their worries and fears and resource them with opportunities to practice resilience, empathy, and communication so they don't become one of the children represented by statistics . . .

But we don't know how.

And life and change happen. Constantly. Death, divorce, departure, diagnosis, and disaster happen, and even when we are going through our hardest personal experiences as adults, we still so desperately want to support our children. But the darn Self-Help section is so big and the Parenting section is so small. And we need tools, resources, and strategies.

In adulthood, it seems, those of us on the journey of growth and healing are looking to make sense of the chapters of our lives in an attempt to expand the plot line. We want to understand the pain, hurt, resentment, and disappointment so that we have the possibility to shift our perspective to one of gratitude, hope, and understanding. The work we do in adulthood to heal from childhood experiences that caused us confusion and grief often feels like taking the pen back from our caregivers and becoming the authors of our own lives. We expand our lens on what has happened to us, work through our memories, and reshape the meanings we previously made. We do the work so we can become the authors we were always intended to be. Therapeutic intervention programs exist, and the Self-Help section is "venti" sized because we know that we want to be well, for ourselves and for all the generations that follow us. We want to evolve so that we can understand our past and heal our future.

Imagine if as children we were given the tools and support to own our stories throughout our childhood? Maybe if we were given the message that we held the metaphorical pen and could write our own life stories right from the beginning we would have a lot less pain to dig through as adults? What if we were given the information we needed in the midst of difficult life changes to make sense of our experiences and create storylines for ourselves that shaped our identities around safety and security?

What if?

In my perfect future, books that focus on raising safe, secure, and content children are the type of books we have sitting on the armrests of our couches. These are the books we share with friends because they "are so good," and they are the books we talk about with our adult siblings over holiday dinners. Instead of the topics of parenting and children being niche areas of expertise reserved for child psychologists, child and family therapists, and education professionals, I envision a future where our children are a *genre* that we are all experts in. In that future, the adult Self-Help section is a little smaller and the Parenting section takes up more space on the back wall.

In an attempt to contribute to that beautiful future, I have created the Courage to Communicate Model. The Courage to Communicate Model is a guide and a tool for Communicating with children about change, which ultimately helps children feel their feelings and emotions while they talk about a life change. It is a method that can be used by a caring adult to give children the support they need to understand life's changes and the resources they need to practice being the main characters in their own life stories. The purpose of *Crummy Conversations* is to give you, a loving adult in the life of a child, a guide to help your child or children understand a major life change and to come through the other side with increased resilience and decreased trauma. The Courage to Communicate Model will give you the tools you need to talk with your children about what has happened in the past, what is happening now, and what might happen in the future. Ultimately, it will show you how to give your child the tools to take ownership over their own lived experiences.

PART ONE

1. THE COURAGE TO COMMUNICATE RECIPE

I joke about how varied my career as a professional helper (meaning I have had paid jobs where my role was to provide prevention, intervention, and education to children, youth, and families) has been, but in all my professional roles, there have been opportunities to listen to different families' painful stories of grief, loss, loneliness, anger, fear, and confusion. Whether I was working in a group childcare setting, as a school educational assistant, a pregnancy outreach worker, a youth drop-in facilitator, a support worker for children with developmental needs, a child and youth counselor, a mental health outreach worker, a key worker for families raising children with exceptional neurological differences, a social work assistant, or a family liaison at a complex care clinic, my hands became full of sorrows, and I didn't want to just hold that pain anymore. I wanted to build a bridge from the pain to the hope. I wanted to engineer a structure that could carry our little people through a change process and fill their metaphorical pockets with resources and resilience. **The Courage to Communicate Model (CTCM) is something for all of us to use while in the messiest of life's changes—without any expectations about outcomes—but with the hope that our presence and our words will be enough.** Often, as adults, whether professional helpers or parents, we want so desperately to bolster our children with resources, but we don't know how. The CTCM is how. This model, this tool, is how we give children the information and tools they need to process, understand, and embrace a major life change. The goal of this empathic communication method is to offer you a tool to learn how to facilitate a conversation with a child you care about that will allow for an *exchange* of needed information.

The CTCM offers you a step-by-step process for getting a child through a difficult change in their life. The CTCM can be used with any life change that occurs, like the Big Ds: Death, Divorce, Diagnosis, Departure, and Disaster. The goal of the CTCM is that by using both the Adult Pre and Post Work and the method for communication, then we, as caring adults in the life of a child, are able to increase a child's understanding, confidence, and capacity for thriving through a change.

When using the CTCM, our desired outcome is to use an exchange of information between an adult and a child to increase the potential positive outcomes for a child, and ultimately, for the whole family.

For the professional helpers in the crowd, we can achieve this goal by using a *narrative therapy philosophy* to empathetically communicate with our children.

For everyone else, we can achieve this goal by borrowing some ideas from a therapeutic approach designed by a social worker and an anthropologist, both from Down Under, to empathetically communicate with our children.

The best way to achieve these goals for children while they get through a change is information and understanding. Helping them know what has happened in the past, what is happening now, and what will happen next decreases stress and increases coping. Any change is a stressor for us as humans, and many things happen to our bodies and minds when we are thrust into a stressful life change (think chemical changes impacting sleep, appetite, mood, behavior, etc.), and children are no different. When we give children accurate and current information about what is happening to them and around them, they can better cope and move forward through the change to the other side.

Every time I look for a great recipe online, after clicking the link Google populates for me, I always move the screen on my phone upward with my thumb so quickly that I have to wait for the page to reload. I hate all the blah blah blah that bloggers put ahead of the recipe. I mean, I don't care that you made this beautiful lemon blueberry cake for your mother-in-law's birthday and that you served it in her rose garden on the perfect spring day. Just get to the recipe already. I put the description of what the actual CTCM is near the beginning of this book in an effort to prevent you from flipping through every single one of the pages wishing you could just Get. To. The. Recipe. However, I can't just share the description of the approach (read: recipe—so many cookie metaphors coming your way!) without telling you who it was made for, where you could "serve" it, and how best to dive in. As some would say, the following is the quick and dirty, but read on for:

- Communication skills needed
- The science behind the model
- What change is and what life changes we're talking about
- Who this is for
- How we use the model in real life!

The Courage to Communicate Model offers you a *recipe* to follow to help share information, and it has seven steps divided into three main sections: the Adult Pre Work (Steps 1–4), the CHANGES Communication Tool (Step 5), and the Adult Post Work (Steps 6 and 7).

The pre and post work looks like you, the adult, working through the following processes individually, both before and after you have the desired conversation. If the actual conversation with your child is the meat and cheese, the pre and post work is the bread on both sides of the sandwich.

The three sections look like this:

Part One - The Adult Pre Work

1. Do your research - Get informed
2. Find your people - Seek support
3. Cull the information - Determine what to share
4. Shape your family's beliefs and values

The CHANGES Communication Tool

C- Communicate what happened
Adult tells child what has occurred that has created a change in their life (emphasis is on the past)

H- How do you feel/what do you think?
Child tells adult what they think and feel about what has happened (emphasis is on the past)

A- And today...
Adult shares what is happening now (emphasis is on the present)

N- Nerves, worries, and fears?
Child tells adult what current worries and fears they have (emphasis is on the present)

G- Going forward...
Adult shares with child what might happen next (emphasis is on the future)

E- Everyone and everything that can help
Child shares with adult their perceived resources and supports (emphasis is on the future)

S- Silly and serious questions
Both child and adult can ask questions (emphasis is on the past, present, and future)

Part Two - The Communicating

    5. Communicate (use the CHANGES tool or communicate in your own way!)

The CHANGES tool for communicating, if you choose to use it, offers three steps for the adult to provide information and three steps for the child to provide information. It is very simple and doesn't require any special tricks, tools, or resources.

It looks like this:

    C - **Communicate what happened:** *Adult does the talking.*

    H - **How do you feel and what do you think?** This is where the adult asks how the child feels and what the child thinks about what has happened. *Child does the sharing.*

    A - **And today:** This is where the adult tells the child what is currently happening.

    N - **Nerves, worries, and fears?** *Child does the sharing.*

    G - **Going forward:** *Adult does the sharing.*

    E - **Everyone and Everything that can help:** Here, the child gives the adult information about their perceived resources and strengths. *Child does the sharing.*

    S - **Silly and Serious Questions:** An opportunity for both the adult and child to ask questions.

Part Three - The Adult Post Work

    6. Feel and release

    7. Move Forward

If it all seems a bit daunting, not to worry; I'm going to take you through it one step at a time. Just like following a recipe step by step to prep, mix, and bake cookies, I will walk you through each step and give you all the tools you need to feel confident and comfortable to have this conversation with your child. The concept is simple, as is the execution. With the right recipe, anyone can whip up a batch of decent-tasting cookies, and with the right support, anyone can talk to their child about a major life change. You've got this, you just need a good recipe. And I've got just the recipe for you: the CTCM.

IF THIS RECIPE HAD A WARNING LABEL . . .

With any model, there are parameters for its use—goalposts to stay within, so to speak. The CTCM is no different. The CTCM is not a tool that can be used if we send our children away from us. We are caring adults who believe that helping our children through a difficult change isn't about sending them to someone else who will "fix" them by doing therapeutic work *to* a child. Healing is about being present for our little people, showing up for them in the muck and the mess of life, and being with them through the awkwardness of change. **Communicating courageously isn't about having all the answers, it's about sharing what we know, being honest about what we don't know, and being still and present for all the in-between.** Could the CTCM be used in a counseling office by a therapist? Yes. Could it be used in a school setting? Yes. Could it be used at home by a parent, grandparent, aunt, uncle? Yes. It is transferable to multiple environments and multiple adults caring for children. The purpose is to focus on communication as one piece of the healing process and that healing through communication can occur in multiple situations in multiple ways—because YOU are the magic.

Healing happens in the midst of relationship, during play, in the everyday moments, and with the everyday people. As Tanis Frame, a Play Evangelist and change-making leadership coach says, "Play is how we're going to tap into and uncover the brilliantly innovative and completely new ways of being and doing that are going to resolve both our global and personal crises."[13] So whether you're the outreach worker, the therapist, the teacher, the educational assistant, the principal, the Early Childhood Educator, the grandparent, the aunt, the adult sibling, or the momma, it doesn't matter. What matters is that you recognize that there is a need to show up for this tiny human (or humans if you have a classroom full of them) and share the information they need. And if you have ever wondered how to do that, I offer this method to you. For all of us, the everyday people.

I communicate like I bake, measuring my words with my heart, and that approach extends to the CTCM as well. This structure is drafted for you to use as a guide. Please follow it loosely, adapting it for your unique situation, your special child or children, and your own style. Unlike in a professional baking course (more on that later), there is no precision here. You can't do this wrong. A little of this, a little of that, omit that, add that: it will all be good. Your personal touch is exactly what the child you live with, or work with, needs, so get in there, get messy, and create conversations free from any fear of judgment, rightness, wrongness, or outcome.

My insides (physiologically speaking) are basically the same makeup as a soft, gooey cookie. I'm all heart when it comes to raising my babies and working with children. I do not subscribe to a "tough love" approach. I'm not a cry-it-out parent, or a sleep-in-your-own-bed parent, or a go-away-from-me-to-express-your-emotions parent. I'm going to stay right with you while you feel all the feelings because there is no human emotion that is too big for me to sit with and hold. Someone on the outside of my world might watch my children with me and think they look like expressive feral ass . . . alligators, but I'm okay with their full expression (for the most part anyway . . . let's not get too carried away!). Anyway, the CTCM does not include any element of asking our children to be stoic, to suck up their feelings, or to cope better with change to make things easier for us. I'm not saying healthy boundaries aren't essential (they sure as shoot are), and I'm not saying my softness doesn't also need a balance of firmness. We must balance at the top of the mountain of firm and kind without sliding down one side or the other.[14] What I am saying is that softness is a large part of what I bring to the table. It is me. Remember empathy and communication? Those are my superpowers (and maybe my Achilles' heel, but that's another book). **This process is about softness and sweetness and love and warmth. It is not to be used to control, manipulate, strategize, deceive, or abuse**. No one wants to eat that cookie, so don't bake with those ingredients.

A SPECIAL SHOUT-OUT TO THOSE WHO MAY NOT REALLY WANT TO DO THIS!

If you have come from a long line of no-talkers, communicating through a hard conversation with a child may be a very big ask for you. As you read this book, you may come up against all kinds of dismissive or challenging thoughts. There are adults raising little people all over the world who have come from families where the family legacy is to lie, avoid, deny, and, at all costs, not communicate. If this is you, there may be thoughts swirling for you like *kids are tough, no one told me anything when I was growing up and I am fine, everyone has some trauma, kids shouldn't know everything adults do*, and also maybe something like *my kids don't even notice what is going on*. And perhaps the biggest blocking thought to this type of communication: *this will hurt too much*. In response to some of these thoughts, I offer that kids notice almost everything. We, as adults, are the ones who don't notice what's going on for them. Kids notice and kids feel. They feel all the feelings we sometimes can't feel ourselves. They may not have the verbal capacity to tell you their thoughts and feelings, but there will be behaviors. There will be a whole boatload of behaviors, and it's going to feel like your kids have gone full pirate on you (read: they become scrappy little pirates of the sea). Be afraid. You know what is the best way to release the pressure valve on intense behaviors? The white flag of surrender? It is the space to express all those itchy, icky, yucky feelings that are brewing deep inside those little bodies. If we can show our little people that we have them, that we can hold them and resource them with the information to understand the situation, the space to ask questions, and the safety of our attention and connection, we will see a decrease in behaviors. **When we show up in the middle of a change experience and say to our kids, with our words and with our physical presence, I've got you and you are not alone, we show them what being a trusted grown-up looks like.** We show them that talking through the itchy icky yuckiness is the way through the change. We lay the foundation for them to get through every change that lies ahead of them. We give them the tools to build resilience for themselves and their children and their children's children. We can change no-talk patterns. You can change your family's legacy. You. Can. Change. Too.

When I think of someone who resists talking about a difficult issue because of how much it may hurt, there is nothing but a hard truth left to share. In the words of writer and relationship expert Leisse Wilcox, sometimes when we have to take a look at hard truths, we need to trust that there will be a soft pillow to land on.[15] Hard truth: Avoiding pain and hurt keeps the pain and hurt inside you. You may think it will be more painful to talk about it, but if unaddressed, you and your child will be left with that festering hurt. Forever. Soft pillow: If you can do the work and walk through the pain and hurt, you and your child will find freedom, transformation, and relief from it. Think of your child having a gaping cut on their arm. If you ignore it because it will hurt you to watch them get stitches, and you fear the pain they will experience from the medical treatment, that gaping cut may not heal. What could have been a small wound, stitched up neatly and healing swiftly, instead becomes a large wound that reopens when touched the wrong way. We must attend to our children's emotional wounds, just as we attend to their physical ones.

As Brianna West says, "If we don't process our emotional experiences, they stay with us like the food we can't metabolize, or old clothes we never get around to packing up and putting out to the curb."[16] Yet when we are brave enough to dig through the extra burdens we carry around, we can reap exceptional rewards. A friend and colleague of mine, who has dedicated her life to supporting children and families and to doing her own emotional work, refers to her deep, dark-inside heart and soul healing as compost. She talks about how it's hard to dig through the old debris from your childhood, but that when you do, you find the richest soil and the most nutrient-dense earth from which to plant your seeds and nurture your future blossoms.[17]

So here we are metaphorically using a cookie recipe to turn our waste into compost so our flowers can grow. Man, life is wild.

And in case you still feel some hesitation about this whole thing, here is the softest of all the pillows when it comes to this child-raising content: Research tells us we only have to get this right 30 percent of the time. True story! Statistically speaking, we can make mistakes and feel like we're failing 70 percent of the time, but if we get this right 30 percent of the time, our children will feel safe and secure with us and learn the skills needed to regulate emotion. Now those are numbers I can get behind![18]

MY EXPERIENCE . . .

At the initial stage of many of my personal experiences with life change, I am often angry, sad, and full of blame (at myself and others). There is no forest for the trees, as they say. My emotions run deep, and they can take over my thinking brain. In the early days and weeks of becoming a single mother, my life was a blur of intense emotions and confusion. I would dream that I was still secure in my marriage and come to the realization of my new reality upon waking up. It was like a fresh cut every morning, for days. I was a mess, and I was lost. I also was defensive and mistrustful, yet I was desperate for some allies in the people I knew and for some kind of road map of where to go. I didn't know how to figure it out, and I didn't know what to do next. My communication skills at that time were awful. I was too full of grief and shock and denial to function at a high level and instead, I spun around anger and devastation and ugly, ugly thoughts. Had the CTCM been available to me at that time of my life, I would have clung to it like a life raft. It would have been something concrete that I could relate to and, boy oh boy, was I desperate for something concrete. Although my child was an infant at the time and talking with her about what was going on wasn't even on my to-do list, I would have greatly benefited from the messages of validation, normalization, compassion, and purpose the CTCM offers. It would have given me a lighthouse in the storm. If it had been available, I would have opened this book raw, defensive, horribly insecure, and in need of judgment-free support. If you could see me in that life place eleven years ago, you would see a shadow of the person who created the CTCM. We are all our parts and all our experiences, and I offer you this look back at who I was to reinforce for all of us that we all start somewhere, we all grow from somewhere. I also offer this not-so-shiny look back at myself to ensure you understand that I offer you this model with a strong and confident voice and a tender and vulnerable heart.

YOUR EXPERIENCE . . .

As you consider the CTCM, do you see an invitation to look at your past hurt? Do you wish you could implement this model for communication without having to feel anything?

KEY POINTS FOR REFLECTION:

- The CTCM is a three-part process involving a pre-communication process, the actual communicating, and a post-communication process.
- The CTCM is about relationship and connection.
- The intervention is the presence of a caring adult in the life of a child.
- Shifting patterns, like not talking about feelings, is possible.
- We must work through our hurts to heal from them.

2. FRESH BAKED (DEFINITIONS)

Communicating to children is what this book is about, but I also know a lot about chocolate chip cookies. To say I have been on a lifelong quest to find the perfect recipe would make something very natural sound really dramatic. I love cookies, and so my love for a good cookie has made me pretty good at making them. They have become a thing in my life—something my children will remember us always making together, something that was discussed on the first date I had with my now-husband, something my friends know me for. I can make a batch of cookies with my eyes closed, and trust me, I measure that sh . . sugar with my heart.

A few years ago, I went to a professional baking class with a wonderful Red Seal baking instructor. It was a full day of baking a variety of sweet treats, and everything was measured precisely. As I stood next to the large butcher-block table surrounded by industrial-sized mixing machines and exceptionally hot ovens, I could not get past the specificness of it all. We had to weigh out ingredients—weigh them, like on a digital scale! As most bakers know, precision is important in baking because unlike cooking where you have room to "play," if you mess up the ingredients in baking, those loafs don't rise. Your golden buns won't proof. Your fancy pants tarts won't brown. The threat of disaster striking your hard-fought efforts for a sugary treat to share with your friends is real. Measure accurately or else, dun, dun, dunnnnnn. To say I spent the second half of this baking class a little bit disillusioned would be an understatement. As I poured carefully weighed and measured white sugar into an obscene amount of real butter, unsalted of course, I suggested to the other attendees that I sorta kinda measured with my eyes when I baked and maybe that was okay. Crickets from my fellow baking students. It was *not* okay if you wanted a perfect baking outcome. I am all heart when I bake, and so to turn my creative expression into a scientific process didn't fit for me. Don't get me wrong: I learned a few tricks, and I absolutely ate every bite of the perfect baking we produced, but my passion for baking with abandon was solidified, and I didn't sign up for future classes.

Baking cookies has been my "thing" for so long that I can't remember how it started. But I do know that it has become a meditation of sorts for me. When I need to process, I bake cookies. When I need to kill time, I bake cookies. When I want to share joy with someone, I bake them cookies. I also eat the cookies and consider cookie dough its own food group. Don't come at me with anything about eating raw cookie dough—I live in Canada where the handling and selling of eggs is closely monitored and cases of salmonella and E. coli are extremely rare. That said, eating raw dough is not recommended and is not safe in many countries around the world, so consume at your own risk. My life is far too chaotic and full of wonder to worry about details like raw cookie dough. Now that I have three small children (hence the chaos and wonder previously mentioned) who bake with me, I have very fortunately and unexpectedly managed to adopt a way of allowing them to enjoy their own creative expression and surrender to the mess that follows. Fifteen years ago I could not have imagined myself allowing three sets of helping hands (that's thirty fingers, my friends!) to throw flour around my kitchen while dipping wet pointer fingers into the measuring cup full of brown sugar. Ugh, kids can be gross. Yet I find myself just rolling with it all knowing the cookies always taste good in the end regardless of the mayhem involved in making them.

Besides my mad cookie-baking skills, there have been a variety of professional and personal experiences that, some would suggest, are more applicable to the creation of this model. I have developed this child-centered model on the back of strong empathic communication skills and on the foundational belief that when children understand what has happened in their past, what is happening in their lives currently, and what might happen in the future, they shift from being the struggling victims in their stories to the thriving stars in their book trilogies.

The basis for beginning this work is an understanding that we're here for the kids and that the skills needed to move through change can be modeled, mentored, and nurtured by us. During life's most difficult changes, we can teach our children to:

- Be empathic
- Communicate their thoughts and feelings
- Practice resilience

As we work through this book and the model for communication about how to communicate during a life change, I explain how empathy, communication, and resilience are defined. These definitions can be complex and cumbersome, and in an effort to keep this read at least somewhat enjoyable, I am hesitant to heave these ideas upon you at the beginning, yet it's important that my use of these terms is not vague.

If you're in a season of life where you are reheating your coffee in the micro-wave three times a day only to find it still waiting for you in the evening as you open the microwave door to reheat the dinner leftovers, then you need very brief definitions. I've been there, and I know how hard it is. If this is you, the efficient and concise definitions found in Option A are for you. If you happen to be in the season of life where you can drink your coffee hot, often while sitting down, then you may have the capacity and the interest to read the expanded definitions. If you're in the hot coffee season of life, the definitions found in Option B are for you.

DEFINITIONS: OPTION A

Empathy – Empathy is the process of trying to understand another human's emotional experience regardless of our own emotional experience. It is not to be confused with sympathy, which is when one individual feels a similar emotion to another individual and often connects their lived experience to that person's lived experience.

When we talk about empathy in this book, we are talking about it as a skill we can model for our children and teach them how to practice as well. Like any learned skill, empathy can be built with practice.

Communication - You and your child do not need to have any specific skills to feel successful communicating because using words to express thoughts and feelings is something that can be taught and practiced. I will show you how.

Resilience - Resilience in humans is built by opportunity, practice, and action. It is not something we come into the world already having within us. Having a structure that both resources and supports parents *and* children to practice resilience and move forward together is the only way to achieve the best possible outcome.

With every life change and new situation, both personal and professional, we have the opportunity to increase our skills and build more resilience for ourselves and our children. Change is an opportunity for skill building and growth, even though it often feels awful and uncomfortable and really, really hard.

DEFINITIONS: OPTION B

EMPATHY IS A SKILL WE CAN TEACH AND PRACTICE

The CTCM is designed with an understanding that communication skills begin with the ability to show *empathy*. In the last five years or so, the term "empath" has become more mainstream. "Empath" is often used to describe someone who physically feels another human's experience, and the term empathy is used to describe the practice of trying to understand another human's thoughts and feelings regardless of your own. There has been some research that suggests that people who identify as empaths may have something called mirror neurons in their brains that help them mirror the feelings of others. Other social scientists have suggested that empaths are people who have experienced childhood trauma and learned to become hypervigilant as part of their day-to-day survival skills. This idea offers us the perspective that if you are an empath, you are working really hard to stay safe by tuning into everyone else's energy so you can determine if there is any risk in the room. Perhaps it's not all one or the other? Perhaps being an empath means you feel all the grays so it can't be explained in black and white terms? I don't know. *Insert shrug here because this is not an academic book and we must move on to the next section.* What's important for us to know is that for the purpose of the CTCM and our work together here, my reference to empathy is not connected to either the mirror neuron idea or the childhood trauma perspective. **When we talk about empathy, we are talking about it as a skill we can model for our children and teach them how to practice.** Like any learned skill, empathy can be built with practice.

As someone who has buckets of empathy, I can match my response, both verbally and non-verbally, to the other person's needs at the moment. This ability to feel is what gives my words value, because when I speak them, you know I mean them, because you get a sense that I understand what you are feeling. When I talk about having a lot of empathy, I am referring to the capacity to be with someone who is sharing an experience and to genuinely and compassionately try to understand what is going on for them. I hold space for all the feelings and thoughts they are having without giving advice, or telling them it will be okay, or encouraging them to get through it.

COMMUNICATION SKILLS FOR EVERYONE

My growing ability to understand another person's experience is what gives me the confidence to tell you that *communication* is the third item that rounds out my triple threat of skills (cookie baking and empathy being the other two, naturally). I am an exceptionally brave communicator. Due to my boldness to speak into the hard moments and ask the tricky questions, I have created opportunities for myself to really hone my communication skills. I'm not talking about small talk, I'm talking about the deep-dive, feel-it-in-your-toes conversations that are easy to avoid. Where I really shine is in the hard conversations facilitated gently. That is my wheelhouse. There's someone somewhere reading this book who ran into me once in the grocery store on a bad day, and they are now thinking to themselves, *She wasn't a great communicator when she barely made eye contact with me while hastily shoving cheese in her basket.* Yes, this is not an absolute. When I am my best self, I am an empathic and compassionate communicator with an exceptional level of emotional intelligence that makes me a wonderful colleague (unless my ego trips me up by making me want to prove myself to others) and a lovely spouse (unless I'm hungry or overtired). Basically, it's important for you to know I have the credibility to write this book, but let's be real: I have my limitations. If communication isn't your thing, I've got you. If you come from a family of no-talkers (meaning people who choose not to talk about feelings), I've got you. The CTCM has been designed so that it will guide you through this process without you needing to be something you're not. Just read on, show up for your kids, and let the model be the magic tool. **You and your child do not need to have any specific skills to feel successful communicating because using words to express thoughts and feelings is something that can be taught and practiced.** I will show you how.

RESILIENCY

Another word that has had a rapid increase in popularity recently is resilience. Sometimes *resilience* or *resilient* gets used as a way to dismiss children's need for support, information, and intervention. Think of all the times you've heard someone talk about how resilient children are. An example:

> Mom 1: "I'm worried that Benny is going to struggle with having to take the bus to school. That's new for him because I've always been able to drive him."

> Mom 2: "Don't worry, kids are so resilient. He will be fine."

This is an example of using the term resilient to dismiss a child's needs.

In the context of this book, the word resilience is used as something we are working toward creating. It is our job as adults to take action to increase our child's potential for success in a new situation. Here's how that looks different:

> Dad 1: "I'm worried that Benny is going to struggle with having to take the bus to school. That's new for him because I've always been able to drive him."

> Dad 2: "Yeah, that will be a big change for him. Maybe there are a few things you could do to help him feel safe and secure on the bus? He'll need some information about how riding the bus works and an opportunity to practice so he can build his confidence."

Resilience in humans is built by opportunity, practice, and action. It is not something we come into the world already having within us. Assuming children will be resilient through difficult change is a way adults make life easier for themselves. We, often unintentionally, ignore a child's need for support and resources and expect them to manage. You would never throw your child into the big pool without a life jacket and shrug it off because you believe them to be resilient. Yet sometimes our society suggests our children can go forward without what they need to stay afloat. The reason so many of us throw children into the metaphorical deep end with our fingers crossed that they will swim is because we are so completely at capacity with everything we must already manage. We're just trying to tread water ourselves during a time when we are expected to work, raise our children, and adapt to constantly changing situations, all while waiting patiently in traffic and smiling with our eyes at strangers. It's a lot. It might feel like it's a lot *and* all your needs for support are dismissed because our society also suggests that *you* are resilient. We often hear that parents can continue to cope with more and more and more, all without support and resources, because they are resilient. If we have adults and children trying to get through a difficult time while both are having their needs dismissed, the probability of a smooth few days, months, years is unlikely. **Having a structure that both resources and supports parents *and* children to practice resilience and move forward together is the only way to achieve the best possible outcome.** While the CTCM is designed to benefit children, it is also structured with the recognition that we cannot support children without also supporting their caregivers.

Regardless of the definition route you chose, A or B, it's important to note that the CTCM is all about the children. Does it go without saying that the model is designed for the sole benefit of children? Just in case that isn't spelled out yet, let me confirm that this tool is a *child-centered* resource. The CTCM has been created for the sole benefit of children with the purpose of supporting them through a difficult life change. If your entire family is in the midst of a move or a separation or grieving the loss of a beloved family member, no one individual in that family will have an experience that is more valued than the others. If, as a child grieves, they punch a hole in the wall, they are not more upset than their parent who cries quietly after all the children are in bed. It is only in this conversation, using the CTCM, where the exclusive benefit is for the child, that the child's experience matters the most. The model is designed so that our adult needs for validation, emotional support, and security are met through the Adult Pre and Post Work prior to having this important conversation with our child. With our needs met, we can manage our own feelings so that we can be completely present for our children's needs.

Now that I've established that making cookies, having empathy, and communicating effectively are my *things* (and in case I've almost lost you with this not-so-humble brag), let me also note that I am not many, many other things. I am not the mom who facilitates the best crafts and activities, I feed my kids packaged food more than I should, my home could use some more structure, and my dog could be better behaved. And my vehicle always has random garbage in it. Always. I will also not sit here and tell you that in my years as a helping professional in a variety of roles that I skyrocketed to the top of the pack as the best of the best. I did not. I have never had a specific niche job that allowed me to climb the ladder of success. It turns out that if you are a stellar empathic communicator, you are really good with people, but you may not necessarily fit perfectly in the predetermined role that is set out for you. Even while never feeling like I was quite in the right spot for my skill set, my professional career has afforded me an eclectic genre of jobs that have given me space and opportunity to practice. While having continued opportunities to practice, what has turned out to be my sword and shield so to speak—empathic communication—my capacity for resilience has also increased. I have crafted a beautiful communication style where I can say the hard things and ask the sensitive questions in such a gentle way that authentic, genuine, and valuable communication can occur, even during the most difficult situations. Toot toot, toooot toooooot (that was me obnoxiously tooting my own horn). **The point here is all these skills are teachable and I have the chops to teach them to you.**

Even with my limitations, my kids have a mom who talks to them about everything and never seems to run out of empathy . . . or chocolate chips. You win some, you lose some. While my professional career continues to be undefined, and my children continue to grow and develop at a pace that leaves me chugging coffee and white-knuckling the metaphorical wheel of life, I have created the Courage to Communicate Model and subsequent CHANGES Communication Tool for how we can communicate to children during a difficult life change including death, divorce, diagnosis, departure, and disaster. It potentially might be all I have to offer, so offer it I shall. You're welcome.

MY EXPERIENCE . . .

When I have been most hurt, most angry, and most scared in life, I am also most impacted by my past experiences. As adult painful life experiences happen, all the childhood hurt I experienced returns to me, and I am more triggered, more tender, and more vulnerable. As a small child who had a perceived lack of safety and security in the world, my being left by my husband was an invitation for all those scared and insecure feelings from my childhood to return. As a child and teen who perceived some experiences as being "abandoned," my being thrust into a separation I didn't choose reinforced the idea that I was unlovable, unwanted, and value-less. Somehow, though, I managed to climb out of that sad and depressing trauma-focused point of view to the one I am writing from today. The truth I had to accept for myself was that the only way through, *was through*. This life change gave me an invitation to look at these old childhood pains, the ideas about myself that I subconsciously adopted as gospel, and my ways of being as an adult that did not serve me. For example, my desperate need not to be abandoned by those I loved the most created an inaccurate belief that I could control people and things around me to stay close. Or another doozy of an example is that my perception of lacking in value and importance created an awful and embarrassing desire to prove myself. Spending years trying to prove my value to friends, family, and colleagues was exhausting. Looking at these things, working through them, and moving forward is the invitation we are given when we go through change. We don't have to accept the invitation, but I am sure glad that I have.

YOUR EXPERIENCE . . .

Are you wondering what you bring to this? As I list off my beliefs about my skills, are you considering the unique skills you may be bringing to this conversation?

KEY POINTS FOR REFLECTION:

- Empathy, communication, and resilience are learned skills.
- We need opportunities to practice empathy, communication, and resilience.
- By practicing empathic communication with our children, we can talk to them about change and increase positive outcomes.

3. NUTRITIONAL ANALYSIS

When I was seven or eight years old, I watched a peer from my school get hit by a car. He was riding his bike across the road at a traffic light, and a little white Honda roared into the crosswalk, hit him, and caused his body to launch over the car and land crumpled on the road in a motionless heap after smashing his head on the windshield. Fortunately, I didn't actually see the impact of the hit or the graphic nature of the accident, I just saw him leave the curb and then waited in the back seat of the car with my older brother while my dad rushed into action at the accident scene. I only remember images from inside my car and a few patchy pictures of emergency responders. I can perfectly describe the color and texture of the seats in our car. I can see my legs hanging down and my feet dangling in the open space where my seat in the back ended and the passenger seat in the front began. Fast-forward eight or so years and my brother and I had a conversation in which one of us mentioned this incident from our childhood. I said something about not actually seeing the accident, and my brother corrected me. He pointed out that I called out and named the boy when I saw him on the curb and then watched in horror as the entire hit, smash, and launch occurred. I saw everything. It took me a few beats to let the revelation set in, and as it did, the images of what I saw slowly showed up in my mind. They had been in there all along. My mind had buried them so deeply that I truly had no recollection of what I saw and was absolutely convinced that my initial memory of the accident was accurate. I had assumed up until this conversation that my memories were an absolute accurate representation of historical events, but what this example showed me, and what I have continued to learn, is that our memories are just ideas and images we gather based on our perception at the time. Or they may be memories based on our brain's good-intentioned protection or on a lack of information and our poorly made assumptions. And sometimes, our memories are based on stories people have told us.

I love this quote from Mark Manson, because it explains my revelation much more poetically than I ever could express it:

> "Memory is not a flawless recording of what actually happened. It's not a video of your experience. It's not a photograph. It is your psychological, artistic rendering. It is more like an abstract impressionist painting of what happened than it is a pure, unfiltered depiction. And it's not fixed—the painting morphs, it fades or expands over time. Sometimes you add colors to a memory that weren't there a year ago, or five years ago, or even collapse multiple memories and paint them into one."[19]

And then, based on flawed memories, we adopt feelings and go forward through our lives consumed by ideas that have been birthed of our own inaccurate perceptions and from stories people have told us about ourselves. The result is that we often become the victims of our old stories and carry emotional burdens that don't serve us.

So why does this matter? And why can't we get back to talking about cookie dough?

The truth is, this is a big part of what the CTCM is all about. **Learning to own our childhood experiences and rewrite our stories with ourselves as the main characters is the healing work we do as we grow up into adulthood, but we can decrease the heavy lifting by having a caring adult in our childhood facilitate the same process for us *during* the life experience instead of *after.*** Using the CTCM to give children information, authentically caring about their experience, and assisting them to piece what's happening together for themselves creates the opportunity for them to see that this is truly all about them. The CTCM is built on the belief that children are the experts on their life stories and their experiences.

Some of you might be reading this and thinking that I'm using a narrative therapy approach with this model for communication.

Some of you might be thinking, *What is she even talking about?! And why do I have to slug through this chapter?*

My husband, whom I really like, has a successful career in the real estate industry. He is very good at what he does and is very caring about the people he works with. Yet his experiences with social-emotional strategies and children's therapeutic interventions are limited. As we've had children and our desire to learn as parents has grown, a book or two on conscious parenting and compassionate child rearing have come into our home. Some are easier than others to read, and the majority are not finished by my husband. He hits the middle section where they get content heavy and filled with unfamiliar jargon, and the book sits unfinished next to the bed. The book has lost its reader, who had an interest and investment in the content. This next explanation is written for him with the hope that he makes it through this book. In the most casual and basic way, I will attempt to explain to the man I love what the narrative therapy approach is, how the CTCM borrows from narrative therapy, why kids deserve to own their stories, and why we deserve to own our stories as well.

NARRATIVE THERAPY

When a therapist helps an adult look at childhood experiences, uncover the problematic stories, challenge old and unhelpful beliefs, and reframe stories in healthier ways, they are often following a narrative therapy style.[20] This type of therapy was created in the early 1980s by New Zealand-based therapists Michael White and David Epston. In a nutshell, the goal of this approach is to help someone separate themselves from what has happened to them and to see themselves as the expert on their life. White and Epston are quoted as saying "the problem is the problem; the person is not the problem," and that really sums up the narrative therapy approach.

There are a few main principles of narrative therapy:

1. Reality is a social construct. Our interactions and dialogue with others impact the way we experience life. Reality exists based on our interactions.

2. Our experience of reality is influenced by and communicated through language (words!).

3. Having a story about a situation helps us understand, organize, and maintain our reality. Stories are how we make sense of our experiences.

4. Due to the lack of factual truth or reality, what is true for us may not be the same for another person and may shift for us over time.

Basically, the idea is that when we experience difficult situations in our lives, we make meaning out of those incidents, and those meanings in turn shape how we see ourselves and the world around us, good or bad. With the support of a professional, we can relook at those experiences that caused us pain from a different perspective and make new, healthier meanings.

HOW THE CTCM BORROWS FROM NARRATIVE THERAPY

The CTCM not only borrows the key belief that children are the experts on their lives, but it also borrows the beliefs that the process between therapist and client, or adult and child in our case, is respectful and judgment-free.

If you choose to use the CHANGES Communication Tool, you'll notice that a technique or two from a narrative therapy approach is also borrowed. At the core of the tool is the idea that we're helping our child put their own story together and find their own voice. This is what I refer to as giving them the pen. This technique in narrative therapy is often referred to as **"re-authoring"** or **"retelling."**

By asking children about their worries, fears, thoughts, ideas, and questions about a change, we're helping children see that they are separate from the situation. They may have feelings and thoughts about a change, but who they are, their personality and character, is not tangled up in what is happening around them. In narrative therapy, this is called **externalizing**.

When we talk to children about what has happened in the past, what is happening now, and what might happen in the future, we are helping children break down the situation into smaller sections so they are more easily able to see what is going on. A narrative therapist would call this **deconstructing**. Using these ideas, the CTCM lays the foundation for our children to consider alternate perspectives on their experience. As they grow developmentally, we have given them the tools to consider their story from different viewpoints, and to make meaning and draw conclusions that serve them best. In narrative therapy, this is called the **unique outcome technique**.[21]

If this is your first exposure to this way of looking at change and difficult life situations, it could be a complex shift in thinking for you. However, please trust me when I say that if we are able to help our children understand that they are the experts on their own lives, that they are separate from the problem and that the situation can be broken into manageable chunks, then they *will* have the nudge they need to make meaning from their memories that strengthen their positive identities, all the while practicing communication, empathy, and resilience.

WE DESERVE TO OWN OUR STORIES

In one of my previous jobs, I assisted social workers to ensure the safety of children. In this role, I witnessed children being moved from one foster home to another, from the home of their parents to the home of strangers, from the home of the foster parents they've been raised by since infancy to the home of a distant relative they have no bond with yet. I witnessed many heartbreaking goodbyes in doing this work, and I can't think of a better example of how we often think children are characters in their own lives as opposed to the authors of their own narratives than on the day I helped force a child into a van. This was a child who had been moved from her parents' home before and was then returned only to be moved again a period of time later. At nine years old, she knew enough to know how this would go. She also knew that her parents did not want anything to do with courts or the child safety legal system. She knew that if she was taken to another foster home, her parents would not show up to fight for her. Instead, they would leave town. She knew they wouldn't go to meetings, or access support services, or meet with their lawyer. So, she fought. With every ounce of her little being, she physically fought against being put into the vehicle that was parked in her school parking lot ready to take her to a foster home instead of returning her to her unsafe family home. She spat, she threatened to vomit, she dug her heels into the cement, and she swore every step of the way. I positioned myself inside the van, just inside the open door. She was on the other side, another adult behind her, and she refused to step in, her hands gripping the opening of the door like her life depended on it. I sat face-to-face with her, attempting to share my calm. I can still feel her primal fear and rage as I type these words. They were palpable. With some time and some gentle words, her anger softened and her tears started to flow. She was able to tell me that she was afraid that she would never see her mom and dad again. That's what moving meant to her in that moment: that she may never see her most important people again. Ever. I didn't know her parents or their long history with the government system of child protection, so I convinced her to get in the van that day by promising her that she would see them again. I promised her that they would go to the meetings and there would be visits planned for her to see them. I can tell you that I truly meant my promises because in no version of my privileged reality could I fathom a parent not coming for their child. My inexperience in this type of trauma and tragedy led me to believe what I was promising. On that day, this little human moved without any of her clothes, personal items, or parents. In the end, she was right and I was wrong. I heard that shortly after the day she resisted her way into the van that her parents left the area without any form of contact information. I think about this girl on occasion and the broken promise I unintentionally gave to her.

Imagine if we had a tool to use to share information with a child in this situation? Imagine if there was a way to show how much we, as the helpers, respect and honor the situation by communicating information honestly and with intention? Would she feel like she owned a part of her story then? She tried to tell me what she thought would happen in the future because she already knew more about her story than I did, but I didn't listen to her. There might not have been choices that could have been given to her, and a different sequence of events might not have existed, but if we had created an opportunity for her to feel stable and secure while in the mess of change, she may have felt acknowledged as a key player in the situation.

It's subtle and unconventional, but by using the Courage to Communicate Model, we give our children the gift of crafting their own narrative and writing a story they own while giving them the power to be an expert on themselves and their lived experience. Giving children information shows them respect, and us wanting to hear their thoughts and feelings conveys to them that what is happening *is* actually about them. Things may be happening around them that they can't control, but when we approach a situation from the perspective of "this child is the most important player in this story," they will believe this too.

In another job position from my past career, I worked as a child and youth counselor. I spent more time working with them outside of the office than inside sitting in chairs, but regardless of the environment, when children and teens told me about their stories and struggles, they often spoke about what happened to them in a very vague way. Many of the parts of their own stories were unknown to them, something that created a feeling of powerlessness and hopelessness. If someone doesn't know *why* something happened, or what happened, or worse yet, what might happen, how can they feel like they have any part in their experience? Based on what I have seen in the children I work with and what I can piece together from my lived experience, feeling powerless, hopeless, and fearful lays the foundation for feeling anxious, depressed, sad, and angry. We often feel like the victims of our experiences. I am not suggesting that horrible, awful, and criminal things don't happen to innocent people, I am suggesting that giving children permission to own their stories gives them permission to see how they can move forward. It gives them the metaphorical pen back, and it creates a potential world with fewer resentful, angry, and sad adults.

Giving children information and space to process their feelings and thoughts when they experience change or trauma offers them an opportunity to view their experience from their own viewpoint and to write their story from a perspective they own. **We are not what happens to us, we are the meaning we make from what happens to us.** When we give children information about what has happened in the past, what is happening now, and what might happen in the future, we give them the tools to take ownership over their own lived experiences. We create an opportunity for them to truly feel *part of* what is going on around them. Many young people don't have a lot of control over their lives, and they have limited opportunities to be part of the decisions that are made about them. They often feel powerless, confused, worried, and scared about what is happening or what might happen. When we give children some autonomy over their experiences, when they have some role in what is happening around them, we give them an invitation to see what happens to them from a different perspective. Yes, most major life changes that children experience happen because of situations or people far beyond their control, but that doesn't mean that they are not key players in their own life stories. In fact, sometimes as adults we forget that children *are* the lead characters in their own stories. They are, in fact, the stars in their own narratives.

I don't know whatever happened to the little nine-year-old girl from that day, but I hope she has found a way to know that she is the star of her own life story. My wish for her is that regardless of what the adults around her failed to provide for her on that day (safety, security, understanding) that she finds her own way to take back the pen (and to rewrite some of her chapters).

We deserve to own our stories too.

It's easy for me to suggest to you that the children and teens who met with me for counseling support deserve a model that will help them own their own life stories. It's also easy for me to speak with boldness when I suggest that children everywhere deserve the opportunity to be the stars in their own narratives, yet I feel less confident suggesting to you that you and I deserve that too. In all my "adultness," with all my privilege and my successes, I hesitate to tell you that we, too, deserve to hold our own pen. But through that doubt, I know it to be true. It turns out that it's never too late to rise through past experiences by reframing our memories and embracing alternate perspectives of who we have always been.

It's also never too late to rise through the muck and mess of life to be there for our children. We may feel broken and flawed and limited by all the things we don't know, yet we move forward for our children. And it's not despite our flaws or our painful childhood stories, it's with our limitations and challenges that we do this work. Meeting our children's emotional needs when we are also struggling means we are constantly walking on the centerline of a two-way street. The duality of deep emotional work is always present. As I write with vulnerability and bravery, I ask you to move forward into conversations with your children with the same. We can be vulnerable and brave for ourselves and our children. And our children can be vulnerable and brave too.

MY EXPERIENCE ...

While piecing together this book, I have come up against many personal emotional blocks. You can't write about yourself, your children, and your passionate beliefs without working through the unwelcome realizations that arise from the writing process. Some are wonderful and insightful, and some are annoying and inconvenient. One such emotional block has caused me to swirl around the idea I am too broken to contribute anything of value on this topic. I am too insecure, too sensitive, and too invested in the validation of others. Sometimes when cataloging your superpowers, you also catalog your struggles, and mine are equally glaring. My tendency to feel insecure bubbles up into anxiety, and my sensitivity to others often makes me care too much about what someone might think of me. And good gawd, I better not be writing this book because I just want to be seen and validated by the world. Oh, the horror. I was recently telling a friend that the whole process of writing this book felt too vulnerable. I didn't really want to put all my stuff out there for the world to see so plainly, but darn it, I feel so passionately about my core message. My wise and thoughtful friend suggested that maybe I needed to fall on my sword for the benefit of others, even if it exposed all the not-so-pretty pieces. It turns out that life is all about coexisting factors. I am flawed and raw and stumble over myself *and* I have a valuable model to contribute to the literature on children's social-emotional wellness. Sharing my stories will expose my blind spots and my current emotional limitations *and* the model I'm offering will still have value and impact. If I am the writer of my story (and it turns out that I am), I can be both vulnerable and brave. I am choosing to be vulnerable because of what you might see that could be helpful to you, and I am choosing to be brave because of what you might see that shows you all of who I am. The process of writing this content and working through my own perceptions and realities has, in a way, given me the pen back to my own life. As I have worked through what I believe and why it matters, I have been writing myself back to . . . myself. There are many people on this earth who know exactly who they are and what they are meant to do here. They have a strong purpose, a clear contribution, and they stand fully in that knowing. I am not one of those people. I have spent all my previous years impacted by my own trauma, surviving my own stories, and allowing my limitations to define me. As I have written, I have risen. Why did it take so many years to know that the story of my life was indeed my own? It's a rhetorical question of course, but it's ultimately a giant leap forward toward a life of wholeness.

YOUR EXPERIENCE . . .

Do you believe you are an expert on your own life? Do you believe your child is an expert on their own life?

KEY POINTS FOR REFLECTION:

- The CTCM borrows ideas from a narrative therapy approach.
- The CTCM believes we are the experts of our own lives.
- The CTCM offers us an opportunity to rewrite our life stories.
- We can create alternative perspectives about previous life experiences.
- We can give our children the opportunity to write their own stories while in the middle of a life change.

4. INGREDIENTS NEEDED

Once upon a time there was a woman working on a book about communicating with children when she suddenly became hyperaware about all the times she had not communicated well. This woman was remembering past conversations with other adults that felt awkward and pointless, when both sides ended up with hurt feelings and misunderstandings. She also was having countless moments when her words to her children were not patient, and her interactions with her spouse were misses more than they were hits. That woman was me. That woman is me.

There's nothing like being focused on a topic to make you become extra aware of how complex it can be. Using words to give or receive information *is* hard. Like resilience, a skill we can learn, and empathy, a skill we can build, communication can be built with tools and practice. With that said, even someone like me (who keeps telling you I am a good communicator) has made catastrophic communication mistakes. My cheeks still flush pink when I think about a painful conversation I had recently with another adult. I knew I had hurt their feelings, but I didn't know how to repair the misunderstanding. Instead of heading toward deeper understanding and connection, the two of us became more hurt, more defensive, and angrier. We ended up parting ways without resolution. It was the type of interaction that could cause me to think, *trying to talk about the hard things is awful; I'm never doing that again.* I have many personal anecdotes from interactions that left me, and I'm guessing the other person, feeling unheard and uncomfortable. There are people in my life who I don't communicate with on a deep level because they are struggling with addiction or mental illness. You can't have an exchange of genuine and caring information with someone who isn't present, and people can't be present for many reasons. Mental health issues and addiction struggles are two such examples, but it is most commonly stress that keeps us from being present when we want to communicate. When I reflect on my wildly short comments to my children or my less-than-ideal statements to my husband, they most often occur during times of stress. I am not at my best, so my ability to express myself is virtually nonexistent. These interactions are uncomfortable experiences that I could use to tell myself that communication is something that I'm not good at or is painful and thus, should be avoided. Instead, I remind myself that communication is a skill, and I use these experiences as "data" to inform my next attempts. It's an easy reframe for me because I have been told enough times that I am good at this skill, so I believe it. If I believe I am good at something, then it's easy to catalog the perceived failures as learning opportunities. However, if you are an adult who has had more communication experiences that left you feeling awful rather than good, you may believe you are not an effective communicator. Maybe you weren't raised by people who showed you what kind words looked or felt like. Maybe you picked up this book and are now thinking, *How am I supposed to talk with my kids about change when I can't even talk with them about their day?* Or *How am I going to talk to my kids about how they feel if I don't know how I feel?* If this is you, think about it this way: Unlike adult relationships, children give us unlimited chances to practice. If we want to learn more, build our skills, and try again, they will give us ongoing opportunities and nonstop grace for our mistakes. Children are gifts to us like that. Prior to approaching this type of conversation with our children, we need to adopt the idea that having hard conversations is a skill like any other skill and that it takes practice and repetition to gain confidence and find success.

My husband is very good at board sports. At midlife, he is still an exceptional skateboarder and snowboarder who can pick up most sports requiring core balance and coordination and just "do them." It doesn't mean that he doesn't fall occasionally, but that doesn't change the fact that he is *good* at them. When he rips down the mountain, shredding fresh powder, then hits an edge and falls, he's like, "Woah, I bailed." Then he gets up and finishes his run. I'm awful at board sports, but that's how communication is for me. I have no natural affinity for balancing on a hunk of wood (wheels or no wheels) while hurling myself into forward motion. Yet when I hit an edge while communicating and a conversation goes sideways, I get up and "ride again." If you don't think you've ever been good at communicating, I suggest you think about something you are good at, like snowboarding, then reframe talking with children as a new skill you are developing. If you experience self-doubt or frustration, go back to the activity you know you rock at and remind yourself that just like [insert skill here], you just ride again.

Marc Brackett is the founding director of the Yale Center for Emotional Intelligence, and he has dedicated his career to his belief that if adults can learn to recognize, understand, label, express, and manage emotions, they will successfully move through difficult experiences, both past and present, and find satisfying lives. Dr. Brackett is also a professor in the Yale Child Study Center, and when he gives talks to parents and professionals, he often starts by asking his audience how they feel. What is revealed is that about three-quarters of his audience doesn't have the vocabulary to express feeling words. Even though it's been twenty-five years since the research and science behind emotional intelligence became prominent, Dr. Brackett continues to find that most adults still struggle to understand, identify, and communicate their feelings. The Yale Center has a crew of scientists and researchers dedicated to teaching humans how to, among other things, "label emotions with a nuanced vocabulary."[22] This type of work would not be happening all over the world if the vast majority of us felt confident in our ability to recognize, understand, and communicate our emotions. The reality is, we are all learning when it comes to this area of the human experience. If you identify with three-quarters of the population of Dr. Brackett's audience and feel lost in how to talk about the emotions that you experience, you are not alone. You are *normal.* We do not have to have our emotions or our ability to express said emotions all figured out to successfully support our children through change.

Communicating with your child is accessible to you regardless of your perceived ability to access your own emotional expression. If you've come this far and realize that you have more work to do on your own deep, dark places, it does not mean that you do not have capacity to support your child. In this case, you can continue to work on yourself and move forward with these conversations. Or you can choose to not work on yourself and still move forward with these conversations. You can desire to get better at understanding and expressing your own emotions and, at the same time, support your child to feel, see, and talk about their own feelings. Or you may have absolutely no desire to get better at expressing your own emotions and can still support your child by talking to them about change. Regardless of which option you choose, while your child will give you unlimited opportunities to practice the awkward and difficult process of feeling and expressing, you can give your child unlimited opportunities to try, fall, and *ride again.*

But you can't bake cookies without ingredients. It would be unfair of me to trudge forward teaching a model for communicating through change without giving you the butter, flour, and sugar. Some of us already come to the kitchen with these skills, but others need to acquire them later in life. I can't say for sure that I can offer you a "nuanced vocabulary" like the Yale Center can, but if you are starting from scratch, the next section will give you a few basic ingredients that make baking possible (read: basic communication skills for expressing emotions during hard conversations).

LEARNING HOW TO TALK WITH OUR KIDS

When I was a teenager, I took a few pottery classes and loved them. The feel of clay on my fingers and the meditative experience of sitting in front of a spinning pottery wheel was very good for my angsty pubescent soul. As an adult, I recently went back to a clay class out of a desperate need to find some grounding as I walked through a midlife reckoning. Clay was there for me, just as it was in the years prior: therapeutic, meditative, and really, really hard to manipulate. Making mugs and bowls, and anything else, takes a ton of practice and a lot of skill. My favorite instructor approached his classes with a casual and welcoming attitude. He had this super chill, super cool energy that welcomed you into his class with the message that anyone could hang out with him and that no harm could be done. He taught his students skills with playful and forgiving words, teaching each of us that it was *just* clay. He met everyone as they were, with zero expectations, yet gave concrete instruction and tools so they could excel at the craft. This teaching style, of welcoming all of us exactly where we were while also handing out real-life learning, is how I approach communication skills. All are welcome, as you are, and here are some tools that will help you.

Long before the internet, cell phones, Netflix, and constant texting, there were a couple of moms in New York raising babies and learning about a new way to parent. After going to a local parenting group, they started to apply their new skills at home with their children, quickly realizing there was a better way to parent than what they were seeing around them. They published their first book in 1973, squashing the rigid and domineering parenting ideas of the times with a new parenting approach that taught parents how to communicate with their children with respect and compassion. These moms were Adele Faber and Elaine Mazlish, and they went on to become international parent-child communication experts. Their work has been turned into a parenting program that is delivered around the world, and their award-winning books have been translated into thirty languages. They were just a couple of moms who stumbled upon a better way of doing things, and they completely rewrote the game of parenting. Long before I was born, they paved the way for me, for so many of us, who believe that the relationship with our children is paramount. Faber and Mazlish taught parents of the '70s, '80s, and '90s how to actually talk with their growing children, and many of their teachings have become second nature to the children of those parents. However, there are still many parents today who, through no fault of their own, weren't given the tools they needed to talk with their children. No one ever gave them the book. So, just like the vibe at pottery, come as you are, super chill, and with no pressure, and I'll give you a crash course in the Faber and Mazlish way of parenting.

According to Faber and Mazlish, all communication between parents and children is built upon the ideas that children's feelings are respected, autonomy is encouraged (autonomy is when children have control and choice in their lives), praise is used appropriately, children aren't given labels, and creative problem solving is used instead of punishment.[23] Fast-forward fifty years and the legacy of their work continues on in Faber's daughter's work. Joanna Faber found that the number one component of the original parenting program that has the most value is "learning the language of accepting feelings."[24] Joanna Faber affirms that all the communication tools are great, but that the magic is the seeing, hearing, and understanding of the child's experience. This is what I know to be true as well, and this is why the CTCM is designed to really and truly put our children's experience at the center of any situation, because it is the heart of the matter.

Faber and Mazlish teach that to do this we must:
- Listen actively by stopping what we are doing to focus on them, giving them eye contact, and facing them with our bodies when they are talking to us.
- Help them give their feelings a name: "You must feel angry."
- Respond with an acknowledgment of what they've shared: "Oh, I see. Wow. Oh, no."

- Respond with an empathetic statement: "I can see how that would have been really upsetting."[25]

They also suggest that we:
- Use words to describe our feelings about the problem: "I feel overwhelmed by all the dirty clothes on the floor."
- Say it with one single word instead of a whole paragraph. "Shoes!" versus "Time to go everyone. Please get your shoes on that are by the door and do it as quickly as you can."
- Give information and describe the situation: "The ants will come if you eat downstairs" versus "Why do you keep taking food downstairs when I've told you not to?"
- Leave a note: Write a note for your child that they can read instead of repeating a request.

They also tell us what an empathic response is *not*. If we are showing our children that their feelings matter, we do not:
- Give advice
- Ask minimizing questions: "Didn't you think that would happen?"
- Give a philosophical response: "Well, life is like that."
- Give them pity
- Deny their feelings
- Defend the other person or other player in the situation
- Psychoanalyze
- Blame and accuse
- Name call
- Threaten
- Command

- Lecture and moralize
- Warn: "Watch out, you might fall!"
- Give martyrdom statements: "Are you trying to drive me nuts?"
- Compare: "Your brother would never have done this."
- Use sarcasm
- Prophesize: "You lied, didn't you?"

Faber and Mazlish offer examples of what they suggest when they talk about *praising appropriately*, and they make the distinction between helpful praise and descriptive praise. Unhelpful praise is generic and unspecific to the child or the situation: "You're a good girl, that's wonderful, great job." Descriptive praise is purposeful and intentional. It is when you use words to acknowledge something your child did in a way that makes them feel truly seen by you. It could sound like this: "You've been working on tying your shoelaces for ten minutes now. Wow! That's determination."[26] This point about praise is really relevant to the work of talking to children about change because it is often these statements from us that teach our children the strengths we see in them. If we are working with our children to build resilience through a change process, they are going to take their cues from us. In a sense, we provide the CliffsNotes, and they write the book. What we notice they internalize as part of their story. We say, "The card you made your mom when she was in the hospital really helped her feel good. That was such a thoughtful idea and gift." The child then incorporates into their story that they participated in helping their mom heal and that their ideas for helping are really good.

In the book *How to Talk So Kids Will Listen and Listen So Kids Will Talk*, Adele Faber describes how the skill of empathic communication helped her talk her young daughter through over seventy-two hours of critical medical care. She believes that in telling her daughter what was happening to her and acknowledging the fear her daughter was experiencing, her daughter was able to relax and receive the medical intervention she needed, thus ultimately surviving. In this example, she truly believed that the skill of empathetic communication saved her daughter's life.[27]

In 1970 it may have been a revolutionary idea that respecting and accepting our children's feelings was fundamental to their emotional wellness as they grew, but the idea is well accepted now. It is also supported by the science of child psychology, the work of trauma researchers, and the contributions of professionals in the field of emotional intelligence. It's not just moms like Faber and Mazlish, and it's not just a mom like me who knows that empathetic communication is key to a healthy human experience, it's science.

MY EXPERIENCE . . .

Going from an emotionally messy adult relooking at my childhood hurt in the midst of a separation to a writer who realized she was the author of her own story was a ten-year process. In actuality, it was a forty-year process, and it is sure to be ongoing. It is happening in a thousand different experiences, in a thousand different ways, and it looks less like a fiery rebirth and more like a boring and very gradual life evolution. This model and my passion for this work had been lingering on my heart and in my mind for many years, but I didn't feel brave enough, knowledgeable enough, or good enough to actually bring it out into the world. I didn't feel like I had the needed *ingredients*. My confidence had to be rebuilt through ongoing experiences, and my interest in what people thought of me had to become less important. As I began to put this model into words and to fill in the pieces that I thought were essential, like basic communication skills, I became wholly aware of my own limitations. I also became aware that anything I expressed during this writing process was also only going to be accurate for this one snapshot of time. I didn't like the idea that my future self would evolve so much further past this, and I had a deep understanding that what I shared here would be reread later (by me!), and I would think, *Yikes, I've learned so much since then*. So here I am, in this moment in time, sharing what I have figured out so far, suspending any self-judgment. What I know so far is good enough because I am good enough. Just as my children are on a developmental journey, so am I. We are all evolving, and sometimes where we are at *is* good enough. And our confidence is built through doing, even though we feel uncertain of ourselves. Sometimes we move forward with our passion projects, our books, our models, and our conversations with our children when self-doubt and hesitation continue to linger around us. It is not the absence of doubt and fear that propels us into action, it is the courage to move forward with doubt and fear by our side.

YOUR EXPERIENCE . . .

Do you perceive yourself to have limited communication skills and emotional intelligence? Do you feel the words and emotions are out of reach for you?

KEY POINTS FOR REFLECTION:

- Basic communication skills can be learned at any time in life.
- Communication takes practice.
- Our children give us repeated opportunities to practice communicating.
- The magic of communication with a child is in the hearing, seeing, and feeling of a child's emotional experience.
- We can build confidence as we practice.

5. MIXING AND HANDLING

One of my children seems to have a deep need for his people to engage with him. As a baby, this little chick of mine was content to be held tight to my chest in the baby carrier, his eyes peeking over his shoulder at the world while I did EVERYTHING. As he grew, he continued to constantly seek reassurance by snuggling close, cuddling in, and tucking in tight to his parents' bodies. In his toddler years, while his need to be close continued, his desire to engage people also looked like dancing on the counter, singing in the kitchen and, of course, throwing, yelling, hitting, and being rough. If he needed someone to see him and validate him and it didn't happen, his desire got bigger and bigger until you found yourself frustrated and upset by something that looked like a child who was "acting out." In primary school, this behavior now looks like a little human who enjoys getting a reaction from his siblings and peers. He loves to make people laugh, to impress others with his trampoline moves, and to ride away as fast as he can on his bike so I have to run in a sheer panic to keep up with him. He wouldn't be described as an easy child to parent, and if one saw his behavior as defiant or intentionally disobedient, they'd likely be at their wits end with him. A year or so ago when we had some friends visiting, one of our loved ones mentioned that it was annoying that this particular child was always "showing off." What looked like showing off to this person was my child showing his family that he is very sensitive to their lack of engagement with him and that he has a deep and profound need for connection. Connection. My child does not seek negative attention from the adults in his life by getting in trouble, he seeks love, belonging, safety, and security in the only way he knows how. When he was a baby, he cried if I tried to untuck him from his safe cocoon in my arms and move him away from me. As a toddler, he ensured we knew he needed our presence with what looked like tantrums, and now he is watching and learning the world around him to figure out the best ways to engage his peers to get his metaphorical connection cup filled. As a parent, I have always put our relationship before my desire for a certain behavior. The family friend who sees his behavior as a child showing off and misbehaving, which can be an inconvenience for grown adults who want to eat a meal in peace or enjoy a conversation, is also the type of adult who likely doesn't think that meeting a child's emotional needs is fundamental to raising healthy and thriving adults.

Thanks to research done by neuroscientists in recent years, we know that previous styles of parenting that involved controlling, spanking, yelling, and removing our children from us (time-outs or similar) are actually the type of parenting behaviors that increase anger and violence in children.[28] Maybe you co-parent with someone who has some of these uninformed ways of being or maybe you are someone who still believes your child's behavior is a personal act of disrespect. These beliefs tend to go hand in hand with beliefs that children don't need the information that this book suggests they do. They also go hand in hand with the idea that adults are in charge and children are here to follow along. If these are some of the life positions you have experienced as a child or perhaps still carry with you as an adult, it may be hard to adopt the idea that talking with children about change is essential and foundational to their wellness. If you feel doubt, trust in the fact that neuroscientists have done research and the science supports how important talking with kids about change really is.

THE SCIENCE OF THE BRAIN EXPLAINED BY A NON-SCIENTIST

Science demonstrates that children need opportunities to feel some control over their lives by being treated like they are the most important participants in them. Children need the opportunity to get through change, and they need a loving and supportive adult to show them how. Their brains literally grow each time we walk them through the process of what has happened, what is happening, and what might happen in the future. If you lift weights, you know that repeated reps and consistent training will grow your biceps. The same occurs in children's brains. With repeated conversations and consistent modeling of how we talk about the things that happen to us, children build and create new pathways in their brains.[29] These new pathways are created by adults who have supported a child to consider their feelings, address their emotions, and adjust and adapt to change. **When we talk with our children about change, we are literally growing their brains.** I mean literally. (To learn more about the impact of trauma and relationship on brain development, look into the work of Bruce Perry and Daniel Siegel. They are world-renowned doctors of childhood neurobiology and neuroscience.)

When I was a brand-new outreach worker for children and teens who were struggling with mental health issues, I received training on trauma and effective treatment methods. I remember two things from that training: 1) what the training facilitator had for lunch, and 2) an MRI image of children's brains. The image compared two brains side by side from children of the same age. The brain on the left was that of a child who had been supported by a loving adult to talk about their struggles. This child had been given tools to work through feelings and emotions and had been given opportunities to practice managing their hard days. This brain was identified as being healthy and not impacted by early childhood trauma. The brain on the right was from a child who did not have a loving and caring adult to help them through the hard days. They had not been given tools to talk about their feelings or manage the stress they had experienced. This brain was identified as being from a child who had experienced emotional neglect. The brain on the right side of the image was half the size of the brain on the left. Half. The. Size.

So, if you need to explain to a loved one how important it is to talk with kids, remember the two brains. If you come up against your own doubts over why this hard work even matters, think about the two brains. On my difficult days, when my connection-seeking child is acting out and I feel embarrassed and judged by other parents who see his expression as my lack of parental control, I remember the two brains. We show up for our kids during these really hard times of our lives, on our hardest days, by working through the CTCM with them. Just as we nurture their bodies with food, water, shelter, and sleep, we nurture their brains by providing them with connection, relationship, respect, and empathetic communication. And in doing so, we grow their brains.

Going through a difficult life experience is hard enough for parents, and I promise you I wouldn't burden you with the task of talking with your offspring about it if it weren't essential. Communicating with our children about change is *essential*. Change and struggle are parts of life, and we can't protect our children from hard experiences. We often have just as little control over what happens in life as our children do, yet we desire so deeply to protect them. We may not be able to take away the pain they are going to experience, but we can give them the information they need to increase their potential for getting through a difficult change positively. We want so desperately to bolster our children with resources and resilience, but we don't know how. The CTCM is how we can do just that, but first it may be helpful to understand the science used to design the model. The key concepts that make the base of the CTCM are:

- All children experience difficult life changes that can be traumatic.
- Being given information about those changes from a caring adult can decrease compounding and subsequent trauma.
- Without intervention, children's bodies are wired to bring trauma forward into adulthood.
- A caring adult is the most important tool to create resilience because of children's need for connection, attachment, and belonging.

TRAUMA

Life changes experienced by children, like death, divorce, diagnosis, departure, and disaster, can be experienced as traumas. They may be the first of many traumas a child will walk through in life, or it may be the second or third change a child has faced. Regardless, the literature on trauma and the body's response to trauma is vast and clear. Trauma has a physiological impact on an individual that negatively impacts their growth and development.[30] I will leave the literature on trauma to the experts (I told you I only have the trifecta of empathy, communication, and cookies, so don't be disappointed that I'm referring to people far smarter than I am here), but I can say in plain and simple language that trauma can mess you up. Trauma can eat you from the inside out and cause you to spend lifetimes sorting through hurt, pain, and fear, subsequently trying to eat, drink, or hide it away. Before you throw in the cookies and stop reading because this just took a really depressing turn, here's the hope story: Even though there is no way around the fact that change is going to happen and that it could be hard, it's actually not the change itself that is the problem. It's not the divorce you're going through or the new diagnosis your child is experiencing, it's what happens after the initial trauma that is often what becomes most damaging.[31] Listen to stories from survivors of trauma and they will often tell you that it wasn't so much the trauma itself that caused them pain but the aftermath of confusion, guilt, shame, and fear that caused a much more impactful secondary trauma. Consider Gabor Maté's statement that "trauma is not what happens to you, it's what happens inside you as a result of what happened to you."[32] You don't have to live through horrific experiences to suffer the effects of trauma.

Academics and professionals who study trauma have also identified that small difficulties that carry on for months and years can have the same effect on our minds and bodies as one significantly upsetting event. The CTCM is created with the understanding that we all live through **Big T and Little t traumas.**[33] Big T traumas are the ones we hear about on the news that are universally understood as damaging to our well-being. When I was pregnant with my first baby, I experienced a significant health scare that involved a potential cancer diagnosis. As a pregnant mom, I endured medical intervention from an oncologist and a traumatic emergency delivery that subsequently created a complex, painful, and grief-filled postpartum period. The result for me was positive, as both my baby and I were healthy, but the experience was Big T traumatic for me and had lasting impacts. Little t traumas are often situations children experience that grab less attention, are potentially subtle, and are ongoing over time. Think of things like sustained hunger, emotional abuse, family members with addictions, divorce, homelessness, etc. Little t traumas in my life have been experiences like helplessly watching my newborn aspirate on breastmilk at six days old and having my whole being gripped with frozen terror while her body turned blue and her eyes bulged wildly out of her head. I slept with her on my chest for days following that incident and was hyperresponsive to every gurgle, rasp, and burp for the next year of her life. Regardless of Big T or Little t, the research is clear that the impacts from both can be insidious, ongoing, and debilitating if left untreated. The CTCM is designed to be an effective communication tool for both T and t experiences because only the person experiencing the situation can determine how deeply impacted they are by it. What may be a Little t for your child could be a Big T for your neighbor's child. If we place the same importance of communicating with our children about a change process, regardless of our own judgment on how difficult that change is for our child, we honor their unique lived experience. **When we honor their experience by empathically communicating with them, we, the caring adults in the life of a child, *are the intervention.***

We become the intervention by giving children the information they need to understand the situations they are experiencing. You don't have to look far to find research that supports the idea that children need to know what a specific situation may look like, sound like, or feel like so they can manage with as little anxiety or stress as possible.[34] Think of the first time your toddler had a sleepover away from you. It is common sense for us to explain to them that we are going to be away for one sleep and that means Aunty Beverly is going to feed them dinner, give them a bath, tuck them in and then be there when they wake up. We often tell them more than once that we will be back in the morning. We. Will. Be. Back. We do it because we understand that separation anxiety in babies and toddlers is common and developmentally appropriate, and we want them to experience as little distress as possible. Talking about life changes is exactly the same. It's just a lot harder because we might not know how. Many parenting experts talk about preparing our children for trips to the dentist, for the first day of school, for their first time going on an airplane, etc. There is a widely held belief that we need to prepare children for the unknown because their lack of life experience leaves them vulnerable to confusion and fear. Life changes like the divorce of a child's parents, a medical diagnosis, or the death of a friend are no different. **Children need to know what has happened, what is happening now, and what might happen in the future because having some understanding of what is going on around them enables them to process and cope.** Giving them age-appropriate information is how we use the CTCM to become the intervention. We have the power to put something between the origin of the trauma, in this case a life change, and the potential trauma of the "after." Our presence and our communication *are* the preventions of the secondary, and potentially most damaging, trauma. We are the buffer, the barrier, the protective factor. *You are the protective factor.*

OUR FRIEND, AMY THE AMYGDALA

Hard times and painful situations can be difficult to read about, and trust me, some of them are difficult to write about. When we read about someone else's lived experience and it resonates with us and makes us recall our own childhood experience, our amygdala can take us back to that time in our lives, tricking our brain into thinking we are eight years old again. The amygdala is amazing but can be a little troublesome sometimes. It's amazing because it keeps us safe by sensing danger and by telling us to run, hide, or stay very, very still. The problem is that our little friend "Amy" can't tell when something is happening in the moment or when it is a memory, so it will send out signals to our brain and body to feel fear when we are talking or thinking about previous experiences. This teeny tiny little almond-shaped region located at the base of the brain is what regulates our emotions and controls our memory of emotions, specifically those related to stress and fear. Besides thinking to yourself, *Fudge off, Amy, I'm trying to live my adult life here*, you can also use tricks to quiet the amygdala when it starts to send your body unwanted warnings. During an especially challenging time in my life, a counselor I did a lot of talk therapy with would prompt me to tell her the current date. For example, Thursday, January 20, 2022. It sounds simple and weird, but it works. You can't be in the past in your mind if you are telling someone the current date. Please feel free to borrow this trick anytime you need it. I'm not a neuroscientist, but the brain is a powerful thing, and our ol' friend Amy is why experiences from our childhood can follow us into our adult lives. Amy is one of the many reasons why talking with our kids about change is so important. If we communicate with our children during the difficult times and help them feel safe and secure during change, we can decrease the potential for memories to root in fear and stress and increase the potential for them to remember these times without their amygdala's needing to send their bodies signals to panic.

When I was working as a counselor for children and youth, I had a caseload of children who I met with for a variety of reasons. As I wasn't a Registered Clinical Counselor or a psychotherapist, meaning I did not have clinical credentials to diagnose a child, prescribe medication, or create a treatment plan for pervasive and persistent mental illness, I saw mostly children and youth who were struggling with school engagement, dabbling in drug use, experiencing tons of anger toward family members, having lots of boyfriend and girlfriend issues, fighting situational depression and anxiety, and facing lots and lots of grief and loss issues. Thus, for the most part, I spent time building relationships and showing kids that therapy was a safe place. My belief was (and still is) that when you have the privilege to be a child's first counselor, you have a duty to do no harm so that when they are adults and they want or need to do the heavy healing therapeutic work, they remember you and think, *Yeah, counseling was okay; I'll do that again.* In my role as an everyday counselor for everyday kids, I bought a lot of hot chocolates and went for a lot of drives. Many of the children I spent time with had complex and traumatic experiences that had already happened to them in their short lives. Their amygdalae were already working really hard to keep them safe, and I saw them freeze, fight, and flee all the time. If I had forced them to talk about something they didn't want to talk about or treated counseling like something they had to do "right," it may have become yet another stressful situation in their lives. My goal was to keep their Amys as calm as possible when they were with me so that once in adulthood, they would feel safe and secure seeing a counselor because their childhood experience of counseling was a positive and stress-free event. Their Amys would have no reason to sound the alarm over the experience of seeking help from a professional. **When we use the CTCM to talk with our children about a challenging life experience, we are doing the same thing: we're showing them they are safe and secure (and their friend Amy doesn't need to protect them).** By meeting a child's need to understand and process the hard times, we keep our friend Amy as calm as possible. Consequently, in adulthood, they can remember experiences without being sent signals from their brain to flee, fight, or freeze. Take that, Amy, you can go burn someone else's cookies.

CONNECTION, ATTACHMENT, AND BELONGING

A child's need to connect, attach, and belong to a loving, caring adult or adults is a primal need that has existed since the beginning of time. This human psychological need can feel a bit burdensome when you're the parent, but it works beautifully for the CTCM. **The parent or caring adult really is the most important mechanism in decreasing compounding trauma and increasing opportunities for resilience for children when they struggle because of the intense primal relationship between a child and an adult. It is the presence of the adult that meets the child's need for safety and security. It is not so much what the adult says or does, it is, in fact, that the adult is there, present and dedicated to the child. It is the BE-ing of the caring adult or parent.**

I can assure you that if we all understood how intense and foundational the attachment relationship is, we may have second-guessed birthing, adopting, or caregiving. Attachment theory is heavy sh**. I say this with respect for something I know just enough about to have reverence for. There are some excellent psychologists who can describe attachment and connection in great detail, but the short and rough version is that the physical and emotional connection between a child and their primary caregiver from birth into the early years and beyond is make-or-break for the child's overall wellness, a fact with which neuroscientists and psychologists agree.[35] There have been numerous studies that have found that the connection between a child and their primary caregiver is foundational and that a break in that connection is devastating to a child's physical, emotional, and mental development. We know this intuitively as caregiving adults and parents, as we often feel it in our own physical and emotional connection to our children. Have you ever felt physical pain watching your child leave you? Have you ever felt a waterfall of anxiety as your child struggles too far out of your reach to help them? Those feelings and physical responses happen because of a primal and other-worldly attachment that happens in our adult bodies on a physiological level. So, no pressure, but we don't want to drop the ball on this one.

Being present and meeting our child's needs during the early years of their lives is fundamental to the preservation of this primary attachment. Yes, this is a day-to-day thing, but it is also an "our whole lives are about to change" thing, so we better show up and be present during the difficult changes that we go through. **When we courageously talk with our children about what is happening in their lives, we both honor their primary connection to us plus ensure they feel safe, secure, understood, and loved in that connection.** Due to the neurological and developmental dependence they have on us for this love and connection, they trust what we tell them and accept us as the experts on the situation. They want us to be the ones to meet their needs and create the safety and security they need to carry on growing up. This creates the perfect invitation to facilitate the CTCM. Simply being present and available and "there" for your child will drastically increase their ability to cope. Do not underestimate your value. Your currency. If you are a primary person and caregiver in your child's life, you hold the key to comfort, safety, and understanding. Your steady presence IS a powerful tool. As you share your calm, as you show up for the hard moments, as you laugh with your child (because kids are funny!), you are steadying your child to get through the change. Think of it as your child being in the middle of an ocean, sometimes floating, sometimes swimming, sometimes treading water and struggling to keep their face to the sun. You are the buoy they hold on to. They will still struggle, swim, float, and swallow some water, but your presence *is* the support they need to get through the experience. You are enough. So, we talk (and we bake).

The other heavy hitter here that is closely linked to connection (but really deserving of its own section) is our human need for belonging. Our kids need to feel as if they are in the same club we are in (not the poppin' bottles kind of club, but you know, the same group). You don't have to look far to find a body of work on belonging and shame research (Brené Brown's books, for example). So much of human behavior is born out of our desire to belong. We continue to strive to find people who understand us, to find safe places to be vulnerable and seen, and to seek out groups and activities that resonate as part of our identities. Adults do this with work, hobbies, friends, and marriages. Kids do it too. They are constantly seeking belonging, right from infancy through their vulnerable teen years (think experimentation and hanging out with the wrong crowd), to young adulthood and choosing colleges, sports clubs, and life partners. When we experience a change in our life, like a death or divorce, our sense of belonging is shaken, if not shattered. As a result, we feel especially vulnerable. **If we feel vulnerable as adults during a change, imagine how much vulnerability change can create for a child?**

Children need us, their primary "big person," to be there to guide them. And in the absence of their primary parent, they need a professional or person of importance to step into this role. They need an adult to support them and show them how they still belong even though a major change is occurring or has occurred. If we can't show up in this way for them and help them navigate through it, they will feel lost in the world. And no parent wants their babies, biological or other, to feel lost in the world. So, we show up for them and we share what we can so that they know we are in this with them—so they know that they belong with us.

(Just in case you're curious, the training facilitator who showed me the MRI image ate the most delicious-looking, greasy, deep-dish, personal-sized pepperoni pizza.)

MY EXPERIENCE . . .

Fun fact about Michelle #27: I like to stay in my head when things get emotional. Thinking about trauma, attachment, belonging, and connection falls in my comfort zone. I like research and academic dialogues, and I love a good nonfiction book about child psychology and neuroscience. My head is a safer place for me to be because my body is where all my deep feelings are. Using science and research to talk about why this work matters and how important it is feels like my nice, cozy corner of the book. It is not, however, where the magic happens. It is where Michelle goes to avoid her feelings. It is also where Michelle wanted to go every time she sat in a counseling office while attempting to work through all her "stuff." Although I genuinely wanted to do my own healing work so that I could rise like the phoenix through the aches of my hurt, I also spent many counseling hours watching the counselor, noting the skills and strategies they were implementing in talking to me, and linking their questions to a therapeutic tool I had learned in school. Although I came to counseling with a high level of emotional intelligence and a willingness to do the work, I also came with an epic ability to avoid uncomfortable feelings. My counselor would gently prompt me to "leave my head," and as I developed an awareness that I would retreat to my brain when feelings crept in (because it was not conscious at first), I began to learn that the times I sought safety in my mind were actually the times when the most therapeutic work needed to be done. So, if a question was asked that immediately sent me into thinking intellectually, it was likely touching on a deep, dark hurt I had yet to work through. Doing this, seeking safety in science, has become a cue that there are deep feelings happening within me. When I want to *think* instead of *feel,* I know something is going on that needs attention. Coming to this under-standing about myself and being willing to do the continued self-work to heal my hurts is why I can offer you this model as a vulnerable person. If I hadn't come to this understanding or couldn't continue to leave my head and move into my body, then I would be hiding myself behind the research in order to keep myself emotionally safe, something that would most likely leave you with content that feels impersonal, flat, and unrelatable. The science supports this work, but it isn't the heart of this work. This work is all about our experiences, our emotions, and our willingness to consider how our hurts and our pains impact our daily functioning, our personal and professional connections, and our relationships with our children.

YOUR EXPERIENCE . . .

Do you agree that neuroscience supports these concepts and validates how important it is to nurture our children's emotional health? Do you disagree?

KEY POINTS FOR REFLECTION:

- A child's brain is a complex web of expanding pathways, and our behavior with our children can either grow or shrink their developing brains.
- Neuroscience supports the importance of belonging, connection, and attachment in the developmental process of children.
- Trauma is experienced by everyone, both big and small, and it stays in our brains and bodies for our whole lives (thanks to the Amygdala!).

6. TEMPERATURE AND TIME

A friend once told me that life was full of 10,000 joys and 10,000 sorrows. This idea, that life is full of highs and lows in equal measure, is something that has continued to roll around in my mind for years. Part of the human experience is living through gains and losses, yes. We all go through experiences that bring us joy and experiences that bring us grief. I don't know if there is any balance to these two experiences, but I have noticed that when we are in the middle of stress and struggle, the pain often feels overwhelming and not very balanced by our previous experiences of joy. When you are in the middle of a devastating divorce, it doesn't feel balanced out by the beautiful wedding you had or the euphoric honeymoon. As you watch a loved one die, you rarely feel filled with joy over the memories you had. When we are trapped in the vortex of change, those painful losses and sorrows can feel so deep, so damaging, and so consuming. If you picked up this book on how to talk with your children about a difficult life change, you don't need me to describe how painful living through a divorce or a death can be. You also don't need me to tell you that learning about your child's medical diagnosis can be a grief-filled experience, or that continuously moving from community to community can be one of sadness and fear. And you definitely don't need me to tell you that living through a disaster can be traumatic. You likely know all this to be true, because you are living it. You are getting through your hardest days, your hardest months, your hardest years right now. Yet here you are, on your darkest personal days, putting your children's needs first. Maybe, like me, you know that as adults, we don't automatically know how to talk with our children about these experiences. Maybe, like me, you remember being a child and not having enough information about a situation to *grow* through it. Maybe, like me, you've worked with children at your day job, and you see that there is a world full of children who deserve better from us. Maybe you just need a simple and effective model, without fancy words, that will support you to talk with your children about the difficult changes that are inevitable in life. As a parent and as a helping professional, I needed a model to help me have these conversations. I needed a resource and a tool to make difficult conversations *sweet.* So, I created one.

I can't confirm that life's joys and sorrows are experienced in equal measure, and I can't deny that some of us seem to live through more sorrows than others, but I am positive that the highs and lows of life in the form of changes are a common experience for us all. I am certain that change is an inevitable common thread throughout lifespans and across cultures, communities, and economic and social divides. We all experience change, and by using the CTCM, we can show our children that talking about pain is as important as talking about joy, and that both experiences are key to the story lines of our lives. Living through difficult change is an essential part of all our stories. And indeed, our children can survive, and thrive, through life's messiest changes.

There are many different change theories that you could study and adopt. There's no right or wrong way to see change. The common theme is that change happens to all of us on this journey of the human experience. Like any of the social science theories (social science is basically the study of people and relationships), someone many, many years ago did research and published a theory, and then people added to that research and built upon it—or in some cases, ripped it apart. University students are often asked to study someone's published theory, then analyze it. That's all change theory is: a published structure of how change occurs, and it can be a fit for you or not. If one theory doesn't fit, you'll likely be able to find another one that does. The idea is that understanding how change works or how one makes change in their life helps create a process you can follow. It's a guideline of sorts, or in my love-language, a recipe. Bear with me while I sound fancy for a minute; I promise this section is short but important. A commonly used change theory created by Prochaska and DiClemente called the Transtheoretical Model of Change[36] presents five stages in the change process that an individual moves through. Professional counselors often use this model to help people shift from an undesired behavior to a desired behavior. Those sneaky, skilled counselors expertly weave a different intervention at each stage of the process to move their client to success. The five stages offered by Prochaska and DiClemente can be easily adapted to what a child may experience. We can apply these proposed five stages (the following words that are underlined) to what a child may experience as they go through a life change they may have had no choice about.

Applying the five stages to a child's experience may look like this:

In the precontemplation stage, a child is unaware that the change is about to happen. They may not understand what's happening or be in denial of what is about to unfold.

Contemplation is when a child sees changes happening in their world. They may start to sense change coming or hear bits and pieces of what that change is about. They are on the cusp of seeing the change before them.

In our work and lives with children, the preparation/determination stage is when we start to make plans for the change that is about to happen. In some cases, this can be when kids start to take steps into the change themselves.

The action stage is when change is happening. As some have said, this is where it gets really, really real.

The maintenance stage is when we see a child or children through the aftermath of the change and into their new normal.

So that's change theory. Boom.

If you skimmed past all that, that's fine with me, but here's what really matters: The method I'm suggesting for communicating courageously with your child to help them get through a change can be used at any and all of the five stages. I give you a recipe that can be used at every stage of change. This method, this recipe, this tool, will create resilience for your child through every stage of the process to help get them through to the other side. I also give you the recipe for the best darn chocolate chip cookies you've ever made, so even if you think this communication method is junk, there could be cookies in your future. Not all will be a loss.

SPECIFICALLY SPEAKING, WHAT LIFE CHANGES ARE WE TALKING ABOUT?

This book applies the CTCM to the 5 Big Ds known as Death, Divorce, Diagnosis, Departure, and Disaster. A better person than I would explain that they can be remembered as alliterations (using multiple words that all begin with the same letter) and leave it at that, but alas, I am not a better person. I sometimes think of the 5 Big Ds as the 5 Big Downers, as in unexpected and unwelcome bummers, so I'm calling them the Big Ds for short. The 5 Big Ds are the especially difficult changes we experience in life and the top life upsets that cause children stress. The 5 Big Ds (I'm saying Downers in my head) are also the life changes that most people experience at some point. You likely didn't get through childhood without experiencing one or two, if not all five. They are also the reasons many children end up seeking extra support from trusted adults, so they are the five I am going to use as examples here. Are there many other life situations that could be in the top five? Absolutely. Am I missing one that is at the top of your list? Potentially. I intend no disrespect by not representing a life experience that may have greatly impacted you or your child. These are just the ones that are at the top of the list for me.

DEATH

Grief is one of the most uncomfortable human emotions. Sometimes we're afraid of it, even when it isn't right in front of us. Losing something or someone we love can devastate us to our core and break us wide open, exposing all the bits and pieces of our insides. If you have ever looked at the face of someone who was recently rocked by grief, you will likely see a rawness so terrifying that you'll want to shield yourself from it. Watching someone in the initial stages of grief looks and feels like seeing the human body functioning with all the light, love, hope, and joy drained out of it. Their body continues to function, but it is just a shell that mechanically continues to operate. They breathe in and out, their eyes open and close, and their legs move them around the room, but their grief is like a darkness that has taken over all the light that usually resides in them. As their world has come to a standstill, they are baffled by the fact that the rest of the world keeps moving on. How can the sun keep rising and setting? How can time keep moving forward? Traumatic and tragic grief is truly the definition of a broken heart, and having a broken heart is something we want to protect ourselves from at all costs.

Whether children are grieving the loss of a beloved pet, a sibling, a parent, or a palliative grandparent, we can share information with them and communicate. We can show them they are not alone and that we are present and able to walk with them through this scary and dark time. Sometimes children are just worried about death for what seems like no good reason. They have become focused or fixated on when and how we will die. They have questions and they need honest answers—and so we must provide them with those. Using the CTCM will hopefully enable you to provide the information your child needs, while helping you communicate the hard parts. When we haven't been given opportunities to practice these conversations as adults, and when no one talked to us about death as children, we are often left feeling vulnerable, unsure, and unsteady. That is normal and okay. This tool is to guide you, support you, and remind you that you are not doing this alone.

DIVORCE

Divorce is a top life stressor for many of us. In my own experience, it definitely was for me. Relationships and family systems are complex and intricate connections that hold a lot of power in our lives. Often, we connect our relationship to our identities and our sense of where we belong in the world. If you want to feel like a bomb has gone off in your life and blown up everything you know, go through a divorce. Or have your parents separate and watch everything you know unravel. As a child of divorced parents, and as a divorced parent myself, I have some living and learning to contribute on this particular topic and yet, I don't feel like an expert. I just feel like I have an honest, messy, and real experience that is uniquely my own. I share my story in hopes that you know you are, or will become, an expert on your story.

What I know for sure is that I would have benefited from more information and communication when my parents separated and divorced. As my parents struggled with the end of their very long marriage while parenting two teenagers, they were grappling with the logistics of this major life change and did their best to tell us what was happening and how. Yet as they struggled to navigate through it all, so did I. My memories of this time are sporadic. Dramatic images from my memory of traumatic conversations and events are like fuzzy scenes from the movie of my life, weaved together without a consistent time frame. I remember walking up the stairs to my bedroom after "officially" being told that my parents were getting divorced. The carpeted stairs were blurry due to the tears filling my eyes, and I put my hands down to crawl up like a small child in a fifteen-year-old body. And I remember how cold my bare feet were on the day my dad moved out because the front door was left open so the movers could haul out furniture and boxes. Somehow, we all got through those months and years. There wasn't a structured plan to move forward, we all just did the best we could with the new normal. I struggled to adapt to the change and became an angsty teenager full of anger and sadness. I went outward with my anger as opposed to inward and continued to catalog the injustices in my life as they piled on. I was a real treat for my friends and family, I'm sure. Remember when I told that story about how my child expressed his need for connection and security as a baby, toddler, and preschooler with big showy behaviors like throwing, hitting, and yelling? I'm pretty sure I could give some examples from this time of my life as a teenager that would look like me as a lousy teen making things generally unpleasant for the people around me with my stormy face and fiery responses to any and every request. Picture eye rolling, door slamming, stair stomping, and a lot of the word "whatever." To this day I despise the term used by some adults that teens need an "attitude adjustment." No, I didn't, and no, they don't. What I was showing my adults with my behavior was that I needed a *connection* adjustment. I needed more security and safety during a time of change. We can't expect children and teens to have the developmental skills to tell us that they feel scared and uncertain as their worlds shift and change and that they need to be reassured that they are safe, secure, and seen by us regardless of what is happening. Children want to know that our connection with them is solid as a rock in the midst of any change. They can throw, yell, slam, and stomp, and we hold steady. There is nothing that shakes our solid stance of love for them. The CTCM gives us a tool to give them this message.

DIAGNOSIS

I am referring here to any formal medical diagnosis given to a child OR to a person they love. The CTCM works for children impacted by a change to their health, either in the short term or the long term, or a change to the health of someone in their life (again a short-term change or a forever kind of change). This type of diagnosis could affect a child's physical health, neurological health, or mental well-being. It could mean they themselves or a loved one needs to have ongoing treatment of some kind, complex involvement with the medical system, and/or experimental involvement with alternative medicine. It could also mean having conversations about helping supports like in-home caregiving or end-of-life/hospice care. Sometimes it's big and scary and virtually unknown, and sometimes it's small, quiet, less dramatic, and common.

When my own child's different needs were first brought to my attention by a caring teacher, I felt an anger so swift and so fierce that you would be sure that teacher had poked the protective momma bear that lives within me. I was defensive and angry. It was a long process for me to move through my anger and fear to a place of grief and acceptance. It was also a long and complex process to navigate the medical system, a formal diagnosis, and the subsequent interventions and accommodations. My experience is one that I see reflected in many of the families I work with professionally. There is a lot of anger, blame, fear, confusion, fatigue, and a heck of a lot of grief. It's not an easy road and it often feels lonely for those of us walking it. I'm almost six years into understanding my child's exceptionalities and I still sometimes feel like that protective momma bear that showed up so many years ago. I also still sometimes feel sad. I can't say that it has become easier, it has just become different.

DEPARTURE

When I say departure, I am referencing moving: moving physical homes and/ or moving to a new town, city, or country. It could also mean moving schools, moving from your family home to a foster home, moving from a foster home to your official adoptive home, etc.

When someone asks me where I grew up, or where I used to live, I often start out by making a joke that I am a well-adjusted military brat. I don't even like the term "military brat," but I use it because it's casual and light and a little bit funny, plus it means I don't have to give them a long-winded answer about where I actually grew up or how many times I moved or what moving really meant to me. They smile, I smile, everyone has a little chuckle, and then I say something like I was born here, then I spent most of my teenage years here, and I live here now. I quickly switch the focus by asking about where they moved from or where they live or how long they've lived in their home. I try to politely dodge the conversation, and not because I don't want to talk about myself (look at me talking all about myself here!), but because it's painful to talk about not having any roots or not knowing what my roots are. Being moved around a lot, especially to different geographic regions in a country or multiple countries across cultures, can be traumatic. It's incredibly stressful for the whole family. If departure is part of your life experience, you may also know what it's like to not get too attached. Maybe you have experience with not unpacking the last box, or maybe you're also skilled at making friends quickly but keeping connections simple and surface-y so that you don't get too attached. After all, why get close to people if you're not staying very long? A rhetorical question, of course.

My now-husband (as opposed to my then-husband I mentioned in the Divorce section) and I have moved together once, and the one thing he knows about me is that as we're getting settled, I have this immediate need to get all the pictures hung up on the walls. I don't want to take the time to think about where they should go or wait six months to see if we move the furniture around; I want every single picture that we have to be hung permanently on the wall. He tolerates it because he understands that it's part of a deep need for me to feel like I'm staying put. Pictures on the walls means security to me, and I crave security (didn't we talk about that enough in the Divorce section!). Pictures stacked up against each other, one by one in a cluttered closet next to boxes left unopened, is an image I don't want to see again in my life. As a momma, I love the idea that my children could come home for Christmas as adults and sleep in their childhood bedroom in the home that they grew up in or sit in the backyard where they used to play. Houses are homes to me, and they have the power to evoke so many feelings, *and* I like the idea of the family home evoking all the good feelings for my children when they come back home as adults.

The irony is not lost on me that I married a realtor. Seven days a week we talk about moving. Our family business is an industry that helps people relocate for work, for family, for opportunity, and for tragedy. My husband is very good at helping people change their whole lives. I've learned a lot about the business: the back end, the front end, and in between all the ends. Of course, because of my sensitivity to moving and its challenges, I often feel curious about how the children of all those families manage the changes they go through in a move when so many of the adults don't even know what's happening. Moving is complicated, and stress is often high for the adults. Big people struggle with the change of moving, both the logistics of physically moving and the emotional and mental toll that the process takes. When stress goes up, thinking goes down, and I see it a lot in my husband's work. I've heard many conversations where people are really confused. They have trouble following information and when and how it will all happen. As adults, we don't expect to understand situations that aren't in our areas of expertise. We lean on the expertise of realtors, lawyers, and mortgage lenders, and we trust those who give us advice. Our children, in the midst of the change of moving, need that trusted advice too. They need someone to talk them through the process and help them understand what steps are going to happen and how they're going to happen. While watching the business of real estate unfold in front of me, I have a general perspective that children are expected to "go with the flow" of moving. They don't need to know the details because they will go along with their family as the change occurs around them. I would suggest that if we want them to bravely move through this change, then we need to provide them with as much information as possible. We need to be their realtor, lawyer, and lender. We need to treat them like they *deserve* to be completely comfortable with the process.

I believe we owe them this in the best of circumstances, when they are moving with their family from one positive situation to another. I also believe we owe them communication, understanding, and information in the less-than-best circumstances as well.

DISASTER

What happens for children when the world changes around them? What does it feel like for them when the environment outside their immediate family home changes in a way that is beyond everyone's control? It's stomach-achingly terrifying. Earthquakes, floods, fires, abductions, suicides, school shootings, and pandemics rock children's worlds. All of a sudden they realize that everything isn't as it should be anymore. Everything they always thought they knew they are no longer sure about. Losing your hometown to a fire or having your home swept away by flooding is understandably traumatic for all involved, but equally so is a tragic accident in a close-knit community. Losing a well-known community member or a peer from school to an unexpected and tragic incident can cause deep confusion and hurt for children. Yes, children are often flexible, and they move through the many ups and downs of their lives like rock stars, but they can also be cut off at the knees by experiencing loss for the first time on a grand scale. When we talk about loss in an immediate family setting, professionals often use the term "micro," meaning tiny. A tiny micro focus at the center of a child's world. When we talk about global disasters and community tragedies, those same professionals use the term "macro," meaning big. So, if you zoom out from the tiny center of a child's world, wider and wider, you can view their "macro" world. When something happens that shakes or shatters that macro world, we have big work to do to support them. The past few years have given us many examples of these types of stressors and global traumas, many due to climate change but also due to hate crimes fueled by racial and religious prejudice experienced by communities in all parts of the world. It also must be mentioned that there are parts of our global community where children have lived their whole lives in a state of survival and trauma. There are children born in war-torn regions who have been trying to get their basic needs met since birth, while being displaced and moved from one area to the next seeking safety, sometimes alone, without anyone they trust. There are other children born into third-world countries where they live their entire childhoods in debilitating and ongoing poverty. It is also important to note that there are children who live in privileged regions with affluence and the perceived optics of safety who are living below the poverty line or experiencing pervasive and persistent physical, emotional, and sexual abuse, all the while remaining invisible to society. Children in all regions of the world can be used as commodities: trafficked, traded, exploited, and used. When we hear about these types of stories happening in our own neighborhoods, it's easy for us to view these as *micro* issues. We blame the parents, or we view the family unit as dysfunctional, but these are *macro* issues. Any long-standing systemic social justice issue that involves oppressing a vulnerable population is a macro issue. All these aforementioned examples are included in the Big D known as Disaster, from the tiny micro disasters to the major global macro disasters.

I don't have any certainty about the tens of thousands of joys and sorrows we all experience in our lifetimes, but if I had ninety-nine problems, knowing how to talk with kids about change wouldn't be one of them. Fortunately for you and me, we have the Courage to Communicate Model to help us get through these Big Ds and all the other changes that are going to come our way.

MY EXPERIENCE . . .

While I dove into the content of what change is and focused on the 5 Big Ds that I wanted to apply this model to, I discovered a curious juxtaposition. During my own process of self-work, I recognized, unpacked, and "cleaned up" my pain from childhood life changes that caused me grief and loss, yet I also felt that perhaps I hadn't experienced enough pain and loss to write about these changes credibly. Would you see my experiences of loss as valid enough? In comparison to others, was my pain big enough? Had I suffered enough? What a curious and polarizing viewpoint to consider a difficult change as something that caused you enough pain and hurt to alter your healthy ways of being as an adult but not to have impacted you enough to be seen as a valid loss. How could I, as someone who has been afforded the privileges of being white, middle class, able-bodied, neurotypical, heterosexual, educated, and born into a country of freedom and wealth, have any credibility talking about pain to people who have suffered pervasive and persistent violence and victimization? I can't. It's not my place to speak for those who suffer this type of pain. What can I offer you is an acknowledgment of my privilege and an acknowledgment that there is no pain and no hurt too small to impact you. There is no place for comparison when we talk about the changes that have hurt us and no point in discounting our experiences as "less than." Thus, I hold both my pain and my privilege in my hands while I offer this model. Without both, I wouldn't have found myself in a place where I could offer it to you, and without both, I wouldn't have had the opportunity to know that all pain is valid, all pain matters, and all pain requires healing.

YOUR EXPERIENCE . . .

Can you reflect on life changes you experienced as a child? How do you feel when you think of them? What type of life change is causing you the most distress currently? What life change is causing your child the most distress currently? Is your child struggling with life changes that happened in the past but continue to be unresolved?

KEY POINTS FOR REFLECTION:

- A change process is an experience from one place (emotional, spiritual, mental, physical) to another place.
- A change process involves multiple steps and stages.
- The same change can be experienced differently by different people.
- The CTCM can be applied to any experience of change.
- This book focuses on five big life changes: death, divorce, diagnosis, departure, and disaster.

7. YOUR KITCHEN, YOUR COOKIES

Here we are talking about change, but really, who are *we* anyway? Well, I'm an everyday mom as well as an every-situation social service professional turned communication educator who eats too many cookies. Hello, my name is Michelle, and I have a problem. Just kidding; it's only a problem on the days I bake. Still just kidding; I would never consider eating too many cookies a problem. And that, my friends, is why I own a lot of stretchy pants. I have spent the past eighteen years dedicating my career to caring for the social-emotional wellness of children, in a variety of professional roles, and my life's work is steeped in being child centered. I'm all about the babies . . . and the toddlers, children, tweens, teens (sometimes less than other days, though, because man, those teen years can be tough!). In my work as a helper, I had many years of listening to children's painful stories of grief, loss, loneliness, anger, fear, and confusion. My hands became full of sorrows, and I didn't want to just hold that pain anymore. I wanted to build a bridge from the pain to hope. I wanted to engineer a structure that could carry our little people through a change process and fill their metaphorical pockets with resources and resilience. The CTCM is that framework. It's something for everyone to use while in the messiest of life's changes without any expectations about outcomes but with the hope that our presence and our words will be enough.

I am also a grown-up human who has lived through difficult and traumatic changes in my own childhood. My parents divorced when I was a teen, and I moved around a lot as a child. Thus, I lacked security and community. In my adult years, I have had times of feeling desperate for security, safety, and comfort. I went through a devastating divorce as a new mom, and I struggle with ongoing fear about the potential grief and loss I might experience in my future. This book is not a memoir, nor is it a compelling story about how I overcame a car wreck of a childhood (that is not my story). It is, however, a reminder that we all have a history, and we all create stories for ourselves about those histories.

Because you are holding this book, you are likely a caring adult in the life of a child. Maybe you're a parent or a primary caregiver, but you may also be someone who is stepping into this important role in the absence of the child's parent. To keep this as short and sweet as possible (and to leave room for unnecessary and obnoxious baking metaphors), most of the writing here will focus on those of you who identify as parents, but I also include a note for educators, therapists, and other caring adults who are considered people of importance in the life of a child.

It is important to mention that it is one thing to facilitate a conversation with a child about something you are emotionally involved in, and it's another thing entirely to facilitate a conversation about a situation you are completely removed from. You can imagine the challenge if you yourself are also feeling fear, grief, shame, and anger as your child experiences those same emotions. Facilitating a conversation as a helping professional about someone else's life can be a safe place, while having a tender conversation with your child about an intimate loss you have both experienced can be difficult. The CTCM works for both situations, as well as those situations in between, but we must acknowledge the tremendous courage it takes to be the parent or immediate caregiver in the parental role who is also experiencing a stressful and upsetting change.

FOR THE PARENTS

Many of us caring for a child's emotional and physical well-being identify as their parent, and parents usually have key roles in the change their child is experiencing. Grieving your own loss(es) makes it exceptionally difficult to show up for your children because during those times you may feel small and scared and very, very weak. As I stated earlier, when our stress goes up, our thinking goes down, and our ability to focus, function, and communicate becomes limited. Our body can be thrown into survival mode, sending all our blood flow and energy to our hearts—you know, to literally keep us alive—taking away precious and much-needed resources from our brains. If you happen to be a parent nursing a broken heart over the death of a loved one, feeling the fire of anger from a betrayal, or trying to pick up the pieces after a sustained period of loneliness, isolation, and loss, it takes a behemoth amount of dedication to your child to put their needs first. When we feel like we have nothing left because life has robbed us of something or someone that we counted on for safety and security, we feel *nakedly* vulnerable. That type of vulnerability can be excruciatingly uncomfortable. If you ever traveled to a country like Mexico and accidentally consumed some of the local water while enjoying a tropical margarita on your sun-soaked vacation, you know the type of vulnerability I'm referencing here. Seriously, if you are familiar with the feeling of third-world parasites having a party in your intestines, you know the level of vulnerability I'm speaking of: you may as well just hole up somewhere close to the bathroom and wait until your brand-new boyfriend brings you some Mexican off-brand Imodium. A devastating and unexpected life change leaves you feeling completely at the mercy of your emotions (or at the mercy of your symptoms as in the aforementioned Montezuma's Revenge example). With acknowledgment of this level of vulnerability and true lived experience for this type of heartbreak, I would suggest that we can use the feelings of vulnerability and brokenness to be there for our children. **Our broken hearts can be an asset in our desire to help our children.**

We don't need to put on a facade of being strong or having all the answers. In fact, this might just be us trying to protect ourselves from feelings of shame and failure. In our weakness and vulnerability, we can show our children the real definition of strength and courage. Dr. Brené Brown has studied and written about vulnerability, connection, and courage for decades, and her work is the top of the heap when it comes to teaching us how to embrace our vulnerability, surrender our shame, and move through life's difficult times with truth and courage. The CTCM gives us the tool to do just what Brown researches and discusses. It gives us a tool to use our vulnerability to create deep connections with our children when they need them the most. It gives us a framework for how to show up for our children, with our real and raw emotions at the forefront, so that they can face their own real and raw emotions.

If you are one of the parents who feels broken open by grief and loss or alone and afraid as you continue forward during a scary and difficult time for both you and your children, know that just as there is so much hope for our children, there is so much hope for us. The beautiful thing about change is that because we are highly adaptable and resourceful as humans, once we get through the change process, all the angst, emotion, and struggle will pass. We have adapted, we have moved through the change to the other side, and we have arrived in the next season of our lives. Those seasons of life where sorrow is at the forefront do not last forever. This book, which I hope finds you and your child just when you need it, will soon be collecting dust on a bookshelf or become discarded on your bedside table. You will find the other side of this change, and you will move forward. And with attention, commitment, and care from you, so will your child.

Alternatively, if you are a parent about to embark on a life change that fills you with excitement and happiness, it may be a bit irritating to have your child not feel the same. Sometimes our intense feelings of hope and relief for our own futures are overshadowed by our children's displeasure at the changes we have brought into their lives. For example, uprooting a child from their friends and activities to move because of an epic promotion at your job. The same vulnerability and realness can be brought to situations where our heart is soaring just as it does when our hearts are broken. Our job is to meet our children's need for information with patience and compassion, and to support them even when it is in complete contrast to our joy.

When I met my now-husband, my daughter was on the backside of three years old. She and I had just found our stride in being a duo, and we had found a lovely rhythm in our home as a family of two. I had finally started to thaw my frozen, broken heart, which meant that I was learning how to have fun again and not bring stress and anxiety to every activity we did. I was also feeling confident in life as a single parent and began to view the whole situation as an opportunity to create a beautiful life for myself, one free of the compromise and complications that can come with relationships. And in that season of my own contentment, the love of my life entered the storyline. Although I had many mixed emotions, including the fear of falling in love again, I was mostly overcome with what can only be described as resounding bliss. Shortly after we became a serious couple, I remember waking up in the night with the realization that he was sleeping beside me, then becoming overcome with this unfamiliar feeling that was parts excitement, giddiness, and disbelief. I would forget while I was sleeping that we had met, and then when I woke up enough to register the situation, it was like a weird high. While I rode that roller coaster, my sweet little bug of a daughter was learning that she had to share me and was adapting to a new person in her life. With time, adding someone else to our duo created many positives in her life, but in the beginning, what was a gain for me was a loss for her. If I didn't pause to recognize her experience in the middle of my own happiness, I may not have had an awareness that any newly demonstrated behaviors or regressions from her were, in fact, a completely appropriate response to a difficult change in her life.

Also, I have no advice about how to meet the love of your life after divorce. I clearly got lucky. I would suggest, however, that you find someone who can source out off-brand Imodium and is all in when things get vulnerable.

A NOTE ABOUT THE SOCIETAL EXPECTATIONS OF WOMEN

I must tread lightly as I attempt to make an additional note here, because wading into complex issues like the historical and ongoing oppression of women is not something I am informed enough about to discuss from a cultural, social, or global perspective. I have not studied feminism, and I am limited in my understanding of these dynamic issues. However, I can tell you that in my life, I have observed that the bulk of child-raising is done by women. My female friends and colleagues still carry the emotional and mental burden of caring for their children's day-to-day needs. Not in every case, of course, but often. I have also observed myself making continued sacrifices in my own life to prioritize my children's ever-changing needs. I have noticed that when I take my gaggle of children to the grocery store and they trail behind me, someone will comment on how my hands are full or roll their eyes at me when one of them breaks down into tears over something I won't let them put in the cart. In contrast, when my husband takes more than one child with him to the grocery store, comments are offered about how helpful he is, what a great dad he is, and what a good job of parenting he is doing. He is given a figurative medal for the things I am criticized for not doing well *enough*. These are my observations. I recently heard a comment, said by a man, that women are the caretakers of the universe. That comment, and similar comments, contribute to the oppression of women by dismissing them and patronizing their experience. It is my observation that some men continue to acknowledge that women are doing all the caretaking while they whistle away on their stroll toward their entitlement. This is worth mentioning because it would be easy for some people to assume that the work of the CTCM is women's work, or that the content of this book is focused on women. If you identify as a mom and this resonates, please know that I understand the burden you carry. If you identify as a dad and this resonates, thank you for recognizing the disparity in parenting. If you identify as a male and think this is my personal issue, please be curious about the experiences of the women in your life. If you identify as someone who does not fall under the limiting titles of male or female, please contribute your perspective, your observations, and your voice to this conversation. We need to hear from you.

FOR THE EDUCATORS

It seems that teachers are either glorified or vilified, especially of late during the catastrophic ups and downs of the global pandemic. You, as teachers, are revered by many as the heroes of the story who take care of our children, sometimes in person and sometimes online, and adapt to the changing needs of the education system with rarely a complaint about the challenges in front of you. Others, and I hope it's the minority voice, see you as the place to lay blame and frustration for children not being able to attend school or for falling behind academically and socially, as well as for the increasing stress on parents as they have to find other childcare options or pay for tutoring and extra support. These opposing views aren't new, but they do appear to be magnified by the current health crisis. Generally speaking, in my experience, parents either feel immense gratitude to our child's teacher or buckets of resentment. We either feel our child's teacher really cares about their charges and is invested in their day-to-day experience, or we feel as if they don't care and our resentment and anger builds. Resentment from parents is only compounded by the fact that we (writing as a parent here) often don't see the work that goes into teaching outside of school hours. We aren't hearing about the lost sleep, the hours spent planning events and activities during "off" time, or the amount of personal funds that gets invested in classroom resources. Like in any profession, there are good teachers, great teachers, and exceptional teachers, and then there are the teachers who should retire from the profession, and each family will experience something different with their child's teacher.

My sister-in-law is a middle school teacher, and as I got to know her after she began dating my brother, it didn't take me long to understand how much she cared about her students. At the beginning of every school year, she spends weeks gathering information about her students' lives, their social and emotional needs, their personal challenges, and their hopes and goals for the upcoming academic year. She asks questions about what pronouns they prefer and what name they would like to be called. She gives them the message from day one that the story they tell her about who they are *is* the story that matters to her. She gets to know them based on what they tell her about themselves instead of meeting them with a fully formed story about who they are based on something she heard or read that was spoken or written by someone else. She is just one example of an outstanding teacher.

As a helping professional turned communications educator, I have an unusual combination of degrees. I went from an undergraduate degree in child and youth care, a program that focuses on child development, family systems, therapeutic interventions, and child safety, to a master's degree in educational leadership, which happens to be a program that focuses on—you guessed it—education. Taking my academic pursuits in this direction made perfect sense to me, as I believed passionately that the key to providing resources and support to families was through education. I've always believed that when we know better, we do better, and we often need more information to do better. I was also fascinated by change theory and how to make changes in large systems, not just the immediate family system, so I went into the education program fairly confident that it was an excellent program for me. I did experience some self-doubt, however, when I learned that I was the only student in the program who was not a certified teacher. Every other student in the program was a teacher who was taking it so they had the opportunity to pursue higher positions within the institutions they worked in. Read: They were working toward becoming future school principals. Imagine a program with "Educational Leadership" as the title being filled with future school administrators? I was stunned. Just kidding! I was thrilled to be in that room with those people. Good lawd, it was like being part of the best club on earth. Sometimes I had no idea what they were talking about, because like any profession, they had their own jargon and threw big words around the room that meant nothing to me. In any given class, I could hear whole sentences that made no sense to me. One student would be talking about pedagogy (a word that means types of teaching methods), while another was talking about phonemic awareness (a term used by literacy-focused educators that means how children hear letter sounds), and still another would be referencing inquiring tools (basically a way of teaching children to be curious). I was way out of my comfort zone and way way way up the metaphorical creek. Even as the program came to its completion and we were all furiously working on our thesis projects, I'm sure many of my peers continued to wonder what exactly I was doing in the program and what in heaven's name I would do with my career following graduation (look, guys, I'm writing a book!). The truth is that my fellow students offered me a ton of grace for what I didn't know and created space for the different perspectives I could share. I felt like they took everyone's differences as an opportunity to learn from each other, and that allowed me to experience how inclusion really felt. It was an incredibly rich learning environment and afforded me an open window into the experience of teaching. It is this experience that I draw from as I offer this model for communication and demonstrate how it can be applied and used in a classroom. I appreciate you continuing to extend me grace as my experience of teaching curriculum to a class of wide-eyed, adorable little humans is nonexistent, so I can't truly know what you are up against as a teacher. Yet I offer you this tool with great respect for your profession and with an understanding that you create little worlds of learning within your classrooms. You lead and nurture groups of learners who are often experiencing struggles as a group, while also experiencing individual challenges, and with resources that are desperately hard to come by. My hope is that this guide offers you a bit of relief from the daily burden that you may feel as the shaper of little minds. Because let's get real: exceptional teachers like you aren't just the shapers of little minds; far from it. You are the holders of hearts and souls and the nurturers of tiny blossoming spirits.

FOR THE THERAPISTS

In our house, it never fails that my children decide to tell me the big feelings in their hearts when I'm exhausted from the day and tucking them into bed. This is also when they ask me the really hard life questions related to world hunger, global poverty, and the magic of Santa Claus. My middle child continually asks me what the difference is between Santa and God, because you know, they both seem to possess the same magic of being everywhere and knowing everything. Go. The. F. To. Sleep. During one of these conversations, and at the end of a very long day, my daughter asked why someone would visit a counselor or a therapist. With one eye open, I explained to her that just like we go to the optometrist to maintain our eye health, and go to the dentist to keep our teeth clean, and go to the doctor when we need a prescription, we go to a counselor to maintain a healthy heart and mind. I elaborated that therapists are professionals who know how to help us make sense of life experiences so we feel strong and healthy in our minds and hearts. I suggested to her that some people think you see a therapist when there is something wrong, but that it is, in fact, a normal and routine practice for overall wellness. That's what I told her because that's what I hope for her, but my hunch would be that if you are a clinical therapist working in private practice, a nonprofit organization, or a government system, you are likely overwhelmed by your client's grief, loss, trauma, and sadness, as well as your own response to it. Do you ever feel like things are hopeless because the system is broken, family patterns are repetitive, resources are limited, and waiting lists are too long? I sure felt that way when I was in a similar role. Being the person expected to not only hold space for the painful stories but also provide the intervention and treatment day in and day out is a very difficult job. Compassion fatigue and secondary trauma *are* real risks in this profession. When I think about colleagues I have had the privilege of working with and therapists I have sat with for my own interventions, I feel a wash of respect. What an honor to be the holder of a safe and sacred space where families tell you their innermost struggles, their deep desires, and their unspoken successes. As I offer ways that the CTCM could be used in a therapeutic practice, I hold the following beliefs close:

Respect for the privilege and honor it is to be entrusted with the hearts and minds of children, acknowledgment that the depth and breadth of your skills allows you to pull from many forms of intervention and treatment, and that the CTCM is an optional tool to add to your toolkit (or, as the case may be, another recipe for your cookbook).

And, they say not all superheroes wear capes, but the helpers and healers who dedicate their lives to stepping into the hardest conversations with courage, compassion, and hope must be the ones who wear their capes under their clothes. With admiration for the work you do, I thank you.

But where do we do this type of talking? Now that we know who we are, maybe we should talk about where we are having these conversations. I mean, we want to know how to talk with our kids about change, but where do we do it? Where do we use the CHANGES tool?

THE MIDDLE PLACE

When I was a student studying child and youth care, one of my favorite professors, Mrs. Leslie Welin, taught a class on the therapeutic milieu. "The what?" you say. I remember being enthralled with her every word but really only grasping the concept on the fringes. All professions have jargon, and mine is no different. I later used the term *milieu* in job interviews and research papers because I loved how smart it made me feel. The base of its origin is from two Latin words meaning "middle" and "place." The middle place. When the word milieu is used, it is referring to an environment or social setting where something happens. A school is an example of an environmental milieu, and a family home or neighborhood would be an example of a social milieu. The word is used to describe a physical or invisible container that holds . . . something. Mrs. Welin taught her students the concept of a therapeutic milieu—in that we could provide support to and intervention for children and families in any environmental or social setting. She took the walls off and away from the counseling office and encouraged us to consider ways to create a milieu of intervention anywhere. Therapeutic intervention can occur while hiking a mountain with an angry teen. Intervention can be finger painting with a group of sensory-seeking preschoolers. Any caring adult can provide support and intervention to a child in any environment because prevention and intervention do not have to occur in only one place.

In my local area, we recently experienced unprecedented flooding after an unusually heavy period of rain. It rains a lot on our edge of the rainforest, so my husband and I thought nothing of it as we bundled our kids onto the school bus in the morning while walls of rain poured down on us. Within half an hour, we were hearing that the highway, the main road the bus takes to school and where my babies were sitting on a school bus, was flooding and becoming unpassable. Our kids ended up being on the bus for a lengthy period of time, sitting in backed-up traffic as they watched the river rage onto the highway and flood the low-lying land around them. Eventually, the bus was able to turn around, and the kids came trudging home with lots of stories of which they regaled us. School was canceled the next day, as extensive flooding closed roads all over our local area. When our kids returned home after the bus brought them to and from school safely on the next day, our almost-five-year-old stepped off the bus at the end of the day and asked if we could bake cookies. It was 4 p.m. and I had dinner to make and lunches to pack, but I said sure because I wondered if it was a request for connection. Yes, we can do something together that feels grounding. Yes, we can chat about everything. Yes, we can chat about nothing. Yes, I can drop everything and be present for you. Yes, we can eat cookie dough together right before dinner. I said yes to all this because one of my favorite professors gave me permission to use my kitchen as a therapeutic milieu. She gave me the go-ahead to offer support when it was needed most, in an environment of my child's choice, because that is where the magic happens.

And that is now the permission I am giving to you. The CTCM is a tool that can be used in any situation that best matches your family and your child. You can communicate to your child while coloring pictures together. You can move through the conversation while washing your child's hair in the bathtub. You can turn down the music while driving your kids to one million different activities and follow the recipe I am giving you. All around us is the "middle place" we need to support and nurture our children through a difficult change.

So, I'll meet you in the middle place, and I'll bring the cookies.

MY EXPERIENCE . . .

Here's where the real butter in the dough of my personal evolution occurred: I had to accept what I brought to the party—the party being life, naturally. My ability to really and truly embrace the idea of feeling my feelings, accepting the pain I had experienced, and living a life of empathetic communication came from accepting those characteristics of myself that I previously wanted to dismiss, ignore, or hide. This blossoming from an insecure helping professional to an expressive writer really got its legs when I was ready to own that my ocean-deep sensitivity and sky-big ability to feel my emotions was actually something to embrace, foster, and share with the world. I no longer needed to apologize for them, hide them, or be embarrassed by them. It also didn't matter if that was the way I came into the world as a product of my experiences or as a learned way of functioning, it just *was*. It just *is*, my friends. Part of how I came to own this about myself was by releasing the other identities I hid behind. I let myself consider the idea that all the things I was clinging to that made me "who I was" were actually constructs driven by my ego's desire to be important and my belief that I needed to prove myself to earn my value. The title of "wife" was taken from me, and the title of "single mother" was given to me, both early on in this evolution and both without my choosing. If you know what it's like to attach titles to your identity and to believe that those titles somehow contribute to making you who you are, you'll understand how dangerous it can be to lose yourself in those identities. If you aren't a wife, who are you? If you are a single mother, who are you? When I walked away from my career recently and walked toward the unknown, it was the ultimate "trust fall." Or was it? It felt terrifying and uncomfortable, but was it a leap of faith or a jump toward my true self? Anchoring my identity to my job title gave me the illusion of security in my contribution to our society. Read: I must have value if I have a job like this. Giving up that false sense of security in who I was opened the door to accepting who I was without the titles. Throughout our lifetimes, we are given opportunities to learn about ourselves and create stories that become part of our identities. I had to work through old stories and rewrite the ones about myself that I wanted. As it turns out, I am a deeply feeling communicator who finds a home in writing. As it turns out, I am enough without the construct of titles or credentials or name tags. As it turns out, I was born enough. And my children were born enough. And you were born enough too.

And that's where I find myself as I offer you this recipe for communication. I was given an opportunity to work through the pain from my childhood, and I took it. I looked at how those experiences affected my way of being as an adult and developed an awareness about how that hurt drove my fears and needs. I accepted them. I then slowly entertained the idea that my identity was something I constructed based on old stories and ultimately let those old stories fall away. I was left with the space to consider who I was without them. When you sit in the gap of what you know and what you don't know (yet), it can be very uncomfortable, but sitting there in the discomfort can be the space you need to find the truth you're looking for. Slowly, I started to see what felt like the true me: less polished, more awkward, but definitely articulate and brave when it came to the ideas I was passionate about. Working through the changes I have experienced in life, both during my childhood and as an adult, resulted in an evolution into the real human offering you this communication model. Without any expectation that you have an interest in involving yourself in a similar evolution, I offer you the CTCM with an invitation to explore change as a form of re-evaluation and rebirth. You can move forward and use this tangible and concrete communication tool to help your children process, feel, and understand change. And if you're open to it, you can use this recipe to enhance and embrace your connection with yourself, potentially resulting in a deeper and more meaningful connection with the children in your life.

YOUR EXPERIENCE . . .

What ideas about yourself are you bringing into this conversation with your child? What ideas about your child's identity are you bringing into this conversation?

KEY POINTS FOR REFLECTION:

- The writer of this model, your intrepid author (sarcasm), is a cookie-obsessed mother of three who has dedicated her career to supporting children, youth, and families.
- The model is designed primarily for those who identify as "parents," but adaptations are suggested for educators and therapists.
- This type of communication with a child can be done anywhere and requires no specific structure, tools, or resources.
- This work is for everyone. All of us. The everyday people.

PART TWO

8. INSTRUCTIONS I: THE ADULT PRE WORK

Almost fifteen years ago when I was working for an Indigenous Nation, an honor that I hold close to my heart to this day, I saw community tragedy on a large scale. The epidemic of loss, grief, and tragedy is profound in Indigenous communities due to the historical and ongoing oppression of Canada's First People (First Nation, Inuit, and Metis). If you think you know grief and loss, hold some of the stories of genocide survivors and you will truly know pain. While I was working for this Nation, there was an incident on a

The Courage to Communicate Model

Part One: Adult Pre Work

1. Do your research- Get informed
2. Find your people- Seek support
3. Cull the knowledge- Determine what to share
4. Shape your family's beliefs and values

you're here

Part Two: CHANGES Tool

5. **The Communicating**
C- Communicate what happened
H- How do you feel/What do you think?
A- And today...
N- Nerves, worries, and fears?
G- Going forward...
E- Everyone and everything that can help
S- Silly and serious questions

Part Three: Adult Post Work

6. Feel and release
7. Move forward

remote area of First Nations land where a house fire occurred in the middle of the night. A multigenerational family lived in the home, and the parents and aunts and uncles had been clamming on the beach during low tide while the grandparents and babies slept in the home. A lantern that had been placed close to a wood stove fell over and there was an explosion. As the family ran from the beach to rescue their loved ones, there was a chaotic scene involving relatives trying to get into the fully engulfed home in an attempt to save their children. Five people died in that house fire. When two colleagues and I arrived in the area in the morning ready to offer support, the ashes of the home were still burning. Smoke continued to reach for the sky as daylight showed the true horror of the scene. I remember thinking that we couldn't offer these grieving families anything. As outsiders, what could we offer this community that had watched a home burn to the ground in the middle of the night? Later, we visited a community gym where family and community members were gathering. Someone prompted me to check on a little boy sitting on the bleachers. The little guy was maybe five or six years old. He was flanked by somber family members, a male Elder on one side and a female Elder on the other. The female Elder told me the boy's mother had died in the fire after pushing him out the window. He repeated to me, over and over again in a monotone voice, that he didn't have any shoes on. And he was right: he didn't have any shoes on. That's all. No tears, no wailing, no emotion. Just one statement for the stranger in front of him. "I didn't have any shoes on." He wasn't telling me that he didn't have shoes on at that moment in the gym, he was telling me that he didn't have shoes on when he got pushed out a window. And that, dear reader, is what shock sounds like. I don't know what I said or what nonverbal comfort I attempted to offer him, but I can tell you exactly how he smelled. He smelled like a bonfire. He smelled like a forest fire. He smelled like a house fire. He smelled like a major tragedy.

As I steady my own sorrow writing this account, I want to acknowledge that this isn't my story. This wasn't the place for me to be. I had nothing to offer this little human or this community. He was exactly where he needed to be, between his Elders, surrounded by his people. And even though it was early morning, other professionals had flown into the tiny community and were present in this gym with us. There were critical incident response teams who would guide the Nation's leadership through this tragedy and the family through their trauma. The loss was both a micro trauma for this multigenerational family and a macro trauma for this closely connected community that woke up to the sound of an explosion and then held garden hoses in the middle of the night while they watched their friends and neighbors lose their lives. I left that little smokey-smelling guy in the gym wrapped up in his community with the knowledge that I had nothing to offer him that day but also knowing that he would need all of us, including the critical response team members, going forward. How important it must be for those helpers to be resourced within themselves and confident in their skills. As they respond to a major trauma like this one, what can they do to prepare themselves to be the intervention?

Section One of the Courage to Communicate Model is about resourcing ourselves to be the intervention for our children. Talking about moving, or death, or divorce, or a medical diagnosis may not be as intense and dramatic as responding to a community crisis like the aforementioned example, but being calm, confident, and supportive is just as important. We can't help our children or the children we work with if we aren't stable and solid within ourselves.

When we parent from our hearts, we know almost intuitively that our children need our calm for them to be calm. We soften our voices when we soothe them, shushing and rocking our toddlers as if they are still our babies, because it helps calm their bodies. Neuroscientists refer to this as regulating.[37] They define regulation as the ability for children to calm down after upset or excitement. Co-regulation occurs when an adult uses their grown-up ability to manage their own emotions in order to assist a child's body to manage. Keeping our adult bodies calm and present under stress shows our children's bodies that they can be calm and present too. In my mind, co-regulation is a way for two bodies to talk to each other without words. What we do naturally to bring our children comfort is a scientific process of using our physical bodies to help their physical bodies stay calm, safe, and secure. And the best part? This act of co-regulation contributes positively to our children's growing brains. Research and science confirm that this act of attunement lights up a child's brain with new pathways that help the child regulate themselves without you as they grow into a big kid and an adult. The Adult Pre Work offers a way for you to plan and prepare for the work of communicating. It may sound obvious, but resourced and supported adults are the first step in creating resourced and supported children. These steps give us a to-do list for regulating ourselves. We often think that talking to our kids about what is going on is the hard part, and it can be, but a lot of what makes it difficult is adults who are unprepared, unsupported, and uneducated about what to say and how to say it. You may have heard the term "front-load" before, and it applies here as well. It is terminology used in many industries to describe energy, time, effort, or money that goes into something at the beginning. The term front-loading is used a lot when working with children who struggle academically or emotionally, because the idea is that if we, the adults, give children intentional support and information *prior* to expecting them to complete a task, then they will have a greater chance of success. Completing the Adult Pre Work is how we front-load ourselves so that we are informed, supported, and confident about communicating with a child. Being present with children who may be in the midst of stress, strain, and pain is really challenging. Many of us tend to want to fix things for little people or prevent them from experiencing more pain—or any pain at all. We want to shield our little people from the pain that we may have experienced or the pain that we know is coming, and it is natural to do everything we can for them. However, that often means we do everything *except* sit in it with them. When I say "sit with them," it could mean physically sitting on the couch with them, but it's more of a metaphorical reference to being present with them through the really hard days without meeting our own needs to fix, heal, hug, or hide the pain away. Having a courageous conversation with a child is about meeting their needs for information and answers, and it requires us, the adults, to follow their lead. It can be difficult to do, so the first four steps of the CTCM are here to support you, guide you, and offer you ideas of how to be prepared and present. If you feel lost in the storm of change, my hope is this adult process will be a lifeboat for you. Climb up, climb in, and ride these waves with me (I'm sorry, but I just can't help myself with these metaphors).

Section One of the CTCM is for you to work through the four steps in the Adult Pre Work so that you can be the supported and regulated adult your child needs. The four steps offer a way for you to plan and prepare for the work of communicating. There's no magic here, but if you follow the to-do list like you follow a recipe, you will find yourself able to co-regulate for your child as you communicate and move forward.

A couple things to note about regulation:

1. The science of emotional regulation in human beings is complex. The brain stem, spinal cord, and limbic system all work together to automatically send our bodies into fight, flight, or freeze. Remember when we talked about our friend Amy the Amygdala? Amy is located in the limbic system. This brain structure works together to literally keep us alive when our brain and bodies sense a threat. The pre-frontal cortex, located in the front of our brains, is "where the magic happens." We are born with an empty prefrontal structure designed to hold the data that we all need to calm our thoughts and feelings and to manage our behaviors. To fill that empty structure, we must be given those skills by loving adults as we grow and learn. It takes repeated lessons and opportunities for the prefrontal cortex to be filled with all the good *data* we need and to "form the neural pathways to sustain those skills." When we are distressed or dis-regulated, our prefrontal cortex is not *online.* Instead, our bodies are thrown into fight, flight, or freeze, and we function from a primal state of being. When an adult works to co-regulate with an upset child, they are not only working to re-engage the prefrontal cortex of the child, but they are also working to continue filling the prefrontal cortex with the skills the child will need to regulate their emotions in the future.[38]

2. On a lighter note, it is also interesting to know that it is biologically impossible to chew and swallow when your prefrontal cortex isn't in charge. Our bodies physiologically can't swallow "when we are in extreme distress." We would choke. In retrospect, this might not actually be a lighter note, but the point is, if we're going to use a recipe like the Courage to Communicate Model to talk with our kids

about change, then we need to recognize that they won't be able to actually eat and enjoy the metaphorical cookies we're baking if we haven't first taken the steps to regulate ourselves, then subsequently help them regulate their own emotions.[39]

STEP 1: DO YOUR RESEARCH - GET INFORMED

The first step to feeling less powerless in the midst of chaos and change is to get informed. Fear of the unknown and confusion in the chaos can be silenced, or at least quieted, by resourcing yourself with current and accurate information. You are the adult, and as we've established, the most important person to your child in this situation, so you need to get as much information about your situation as possible. Turn to Google, call a friend, take a step in one direction to get information about the situation you've found yourself in. Put on your detective hat and ask all the questions. Approach trusted friends or colleagues who have walked the path before you. You don't have to provide information to seek information. Follow the trail you are given. An idea from one person will lead to another idea, and so on. If we believe that change is the one similarity in all our lives, then there are others before you who will have experienced something similar. Capitalize on their experiences and take all the gems from their missteps, their successes, and their "I wish I had knowns."

This step was particularly important for me when my own child was diagnosed as having a neurodivergent brain, meaning her brain functions in a way that it is not considered "normal."[40] My child was perfectly imperfect to me, and I had never entertained the possibility that something could be *wrong* with her. When she was first diagnosed, I felt lost, confused, alone, and defeated. It's a lousy combination to feel both anger and sadness about something, while also feeling overwhelmed about not knowing what exactly you are supposed to do about it. It's like being given just enough information to know that everything is not as it should be, but not being given enough information to know what any of it means for you or your family.

And that is where many of us find ourselves at the beginning of the CTCM. It is where I found myself. Years out from this moment in time, and as I write these words now, I can still feel the lost-ness I felt at the time, although I can't explain to you what I was grieving *exactly* or why I sometimes still feel that grief. I can say, though, that wading into this work of getting informed and being your child's source of information takes ongoing energy and ongoing bravery. It's for the brave mommas. It's for the brave daddies. It's for the brave grandparents. It's for the brave ones. There's a reason many people avoid having the hard conversations: maybe if we don't talk about it, maybe if we don't know about it *for sure*, then it's not there. Maybe it's not happening.

Whether we're using my story of learning about my child's neurological differences (her gorgeous brain!), or we have just lost a loved one, been told we have to relocate for work, or have been handed divorce paperwork, learning all you can about the situation you are in gives you something to hold on to. It gives you facts and research and concrete data to fill your mind with while you process this new information. It gives you the opportunity to take action. So, search the internet, go to the library, phone a friend, contact professionals, dig through social media, and get on with the task of finding out the things you need to know.

STEP 2: FIND YOUR PEOPLE - SEEK SUPPORT

Yes, change is something we all experience, and yes, death, divorce, diagnosis, departure, and disaster are all common lived experiences, but finding your people isn't about finding other people who had the same experience. It's about finding people who have had a similar experience *who you can relate to and connect with.* While you've been researching and gathering knowledge, you will have come across a wide variety of people, and those people are all going to handle things differently. In this step in the process, we are looking for people who we can see ourselves in and who we can also be mentored under. Someone (or a group of people) who have walked the road before us who can point out the potholes and cheer us on when we get tired of the walk. You get it. Find your people.

Even if you are a highly independent, very private introvert who prefers to go the road of life alone, I encourage you to find at least one support person to help you. A trusted friend, colleague, or professional (yes, you can pay someone to support you) that you can check in with throughout this life change. In this step, we find our people or our person, so that we have the support and resources we need to create a safe space for a child.

As of this writing, we are in year two of a global pandemic, and the impacts are being felt far and wide. For many, we have experienced an ongoing trauma in the form of a global **disaster**. Depending on what part of the world you live in, the pandemic may have affected you and your life differently, but from my corner of the world, I've seen a lot of change. Parents who are stretched so thin they are barely coping. Adults who are reevaluating their entire careers, relationships, sexual orientation, life goals, and beliefs and values. Seniors who are isolated from their communities like never before. Teeny tiny little people who are missing major developmental milestones because they aren't able to read expressions and facial cues because the adults around them have faces that are often covered in masks. Preschool-aged children who are unsure how to play, to share, to problem solve because they haven't been given the opportunities to practice. School-aged children who are adapting to online learning and then back to classroom learning and then back to online learning again. It has been months and months of sustained chronic stress, and it is deteriorating minds, bodies, marriages, friendships, careers, and livelihoods. As it has evolved, the division in our families and communities, which started as a sliver of difference, has expanded into a deep chasm of differences. With the implementation of vaccinations, some mandatory for certain industries, as well as the requirement of vaccine passports, the controversy has become polarizing. So as a global community, we have been experiencing chronic and ongoing stress in a climate of increasing conflict with real-life consequences depending on how our beliefs and values have driven our decisions.

Finding our people (or our person) has never been more important. We have needed contact with someone—a friend, a family member, someone in our bubble—with whom we can vent, talk, complain, and celebrate. We have all needed someone who we can relate to and who understands our challenges. We have needed support. And for those of us who haven't had it due to extreme isolation, there has most certainly been an increase in depression, anxiety, family breakdowns, suicide, etc. The lives we are all currently living show how our wellness depends on our connection to others. We are social beings, and we need our people.

STEP 3: CULL THE INFORMATION - DETERMINE WHAT TO SHARE

So, we're drowning in resources and information, and we have our support person, and now we must figure out what information actually matters to *us*. This is a really important step because there is going to be information swimming around in your head that doesn't apply to your specific situation or won't fit for your child's age and stage. Just like a photographer who goes home from a shoot and culls their photos, editing out the blurry and rough images, this step calls for you to cull the information you've gained that doesn't fit for you. Get really clear on what information you want to share with your child: information that is specific to your child's unique change and specific to your child's ability to both process and understand it. This is about them after all, so this step requires you to put aside the information you need to know for yourself and your own understanding and bring forward the information you want your child to know.

This is also the time to determine the information that you do not want to share with your child. You are allowed to determine what isn't appropriate for this time of their life. Some details can and need to be saved for an older developmental stage. If you start to feel like it is hard and overwhelming, sift through and decide what you are (and what you are not) bringing forward, and please let me remind you that there is no right way to do it. Everything about this method is simply a guideline for you to follow—a suggested recipe for communication, not a rule book. You follow it as loosely as suits you, with your own contributions and omissions as necessary.

When I was in my early twenties, I was dating a lovely boy who was also in his early twenties. It was the kind of relationship where you're all in and it feels all amazing and chemical and intoxicating. We found our way together for about six months. I remember meeting him after work one day and bringing him a fresh batch of cookies (I told you that cookies have been my thing for a long time!). He happened to be enrolled in a proper university culinary arts program and was being schooled on all things professional in the kitchen. While sitting in my car in the parking lot of his place of employment, he took a bite out of one of the cookies and made a comment that cookies were supposed to be round. Excuse me? Turns out that's what you learn in professional programs: cookies are supposed to be round. Shortly after the "cookie in car" incident, I started scooping my cookie dough with perfectly sized ice cream scoops. To this day, I refer to ice cream scoops as cookie scoops and keep a jar full of different sized scoops in my cupboard. Take that, round cookies for life mother fuc . . . friend. My point here (there is one, I promise) is why do cookies have to be round? They don't. We don't need more institutions, more teachers, and more rule books telling us how something "should" be. Do cookies taste better if they are perfectly round? Hardly. And even though I measure my cookie dough now, I can tell you that I would take an awkwardly shaped yet delicious cookie over a dry, cakey, not-so-delicious, perfectly round cookie any day of the week. You do *you* during this process. No judgment. There is no one here who is going to tell you that your cookies are supposed to be round.

STEP 4: SHAPE YOUR FAMILY'S BELIEFS AND VALUES

Another fundamental step is shaping our beliefs and values. This is a really important step because we often don't consider what our values are on a topic until we get asked about them. If we're opening this type of conversation with a child, they are going to ask the questions and they deserve honest answers. You may have clarity on your broader values and beliefs (think religion, education, health care, politics), but this is the opportunity to get really clear on your values and beliefs as they connect to the conversation at hand.

For those of us in the middle of a separation or divorce, this step is probably at the forefront of your mind. Divorce is confusing for everyone, the adults and children alike, and everyone wants answers at the same time. Often, what we previously believed about life may be shifting, or we may feel like everything that was a "for sure" before is now a giant unknown. In reflecting on my own experience of divorce, it's likely that as a young adult, I was pretty desperate to create my own family. Not that I had any awareness of it at the time, but my hunch is that I was desperate to create the security I missed from my early childhood when my family unit was intact. I really had no idea what real love looked or felt like, but I sure was keen to be wanted by someone in the most secure and solid way possible. The idea of creating a marriage and family that was forever was very important to me. So, I got married, not too young, not too quickly, but without any way to know my own desperation and without any awareness of my own deep and primal need to belong. I went into that marriage terrified of divorce and completely focused on doing things *right*. My life's mission was to be dedicated to my marriage. Forever. But that's not what marriage and family is about. It's not supposed to be about your need to belong to something for the sake of security and identity. That's no foundation for building a life. It's no surprise that as my very short first marriage unraveled, it looked a lot like trying to hold sand in my hands as it ran through my fingers. Let me tell you, clinging to my husband and our crumbling marriage was absolutely like trying to catch the waves as they rolled away from me back to the deep, dark ocean. As he broke away from me, I only became more desperate and more panicked, digging in my heels on the shore of our life together, trying everything I knew to hold on to someone and something that was never meant for me. I was trying to keep the illusion of security and safety that I was so desperate to have. We were separated before our second anniversary, and as I rocked our new baby in my arms and stared at the walls of my empty house, I felt a loss like I never imagined. It was incredibly unfair of me to shovel all my *expectations* for safety and security onto my ex-husband's shoulders, but I subconsciously did it anyway. Funny how life gives you the opportunity to face your biggest fears and come out the other side, isn't it? It's not funny at all of course, but it is very cathartic. When it all falls apart, there's nothing to do but clean up your own mess and put the pieces of yourself back together.

It's been many years now, and that tiny baby in my arms is now a thriving preteen. Although she doesn't have any experiences or memories of her parents living in the same house as a family unit, she still holds that original family close in her heart. You'd think she wouldn't know anything different from having separated parents, but she crafted the memories for herself and uses her imagination to picture her two biological parents living with her as a secure family unit. In our experience of a family breakdown, we, as her parents, were spared from explaining to her the logistics of our separation because she was an infant. We were able to avoid the painful and awkward discussion of why and how and who and when, but those questions come up, and as she grows, she continues to want to understand. Part of her wants to know our story because she believes it is her story too, and it connects her to who she is in the world. I have stumbled through her questions, shying away from the whole truth in my attempts to protect her. I often frame things in the simple concept of friendly love versus romantic love, but simple answers aren't going to work forever. She knows breakups aren't usually mutual, that heartache happens, and that these things can be complex adult issues, so I have to continue to bring my courage to these conversations. I have to continue to touch on a time in my life that was hurtful and sad, and I will have to continue to do it as she grows into knowing adult issues. I need to continue to gain clarity on my values and beliefs so that I can draw from them as I answer her ongoing questions.

As we make sense of our human experience and shape our beliefs and values, we are then able to help our children make sense of their human experience. Major life changes, like death of a loved one or parental divorce, are the types of painful experiences that drive us to seek answers to our questions. Once we know our beliefs and values, we can facilitate an open, honest conversation that gives our children all the information they need to walk forward without the burden of misunderstanding and misinformation.

And then we get to doing the talking. Finally, right?

AMANDA'S EXPERIENCE . . .

In January 2021, I was so focused on making the most of every single moment with my terminally ill dad that it nearly knocked me off my feet when we discovered our family pet had also been taken down by cancer. Little Beauski Beau, our feisty miniature pinscher who had ruled our lives for just over a decade, went out of this world just like he lived in it: fast and furious. It was a whirlwind week of vet trips, testing, and worry before we had to make the heartbreaking decision to say goodbye and end his suffering.

Up until then, our son had not known a day without Beau. My background is in child and youth care, and so I often think this helps me be more prepared for handling difficult situations with my son in the wisest of ways, but that seems to be more of a fake news reel. When you are in it, you just have to do the best you can with the resources you have, and textbooks or theoretical frameworks just do not prepare you for simultaneously snuggling your boy and your pup while explaining to them that it is the last day to do so.

My husband and I knew the importance of speaking openly with our son about what was happening and did not try to hide our own sorrow at the situation. Our son was curious and had questions, so we tried our best to answer honestly while also being mindful that there were some details beyond his years. We talked about how grateful we were for all the many years we had Beau, we looked at pictures, and we shared stories and laughed at all his crazy quirks we would miss.

But even as prepared as we tried to be, the first day we entered our home without Beau there click-clacking his nails on the hardwood to greet us, our son was confused. It is just too much for the brain to comprehend the finality of death, and so even as you work so hard to prepare, those fight-or-flight sensors in the brain attempt to wish it all away. He asked us questions about where

Beau had gone and when he would be back. We answered as best we could, and we held him as he cried. We cried too, and we talked a lot about how it is okay to have big feelings because losing Beau was a very big deal for all of us. As the days moved on, the questions faded, and he seemed to begin to understand that Beau would not be coming back.

Four months later, my son had to say goodbye to his grandpa. Although that loss was colossal on the scale of grief for an eight-year-old, Beau had given a gift to all of us in preparation of it. He had helped us learn how to grieve together as a family and had shown us our own strengths and resilience in moving forward beyond the unimaginable. So, although the feelings about losing Grandpa were different, they had just enough familiarity that we could take those deep breaths and know we could and would survive this loss.

Amanda is an empathic communicator who has more than twenty years' experience in the field of child safety. More recently, she discovered the true complexities of parenting when she became a mom to a (now) eight-year-old boy.

YOUR EXPERIENCE . . .

If you are in the middle of a life change or are working with a child experiencing one, apply the first four steps of the CTCM to your specific situation.

1.   Do your research: Get informed

I can take steps to gather information by _____

_____

I'd really like to know more about _____

_____

The things I already know are _____

_____

2.   Seek support: Find your people

The person who I would like to support me is _____

_____

One other person I could lean on if I need to is _____

_____

The type of support that feels good to me looks like _____

_____

3.   Cull the information: Determine what to share

The two things I want to tell my child are _____

_____

One thing my child is not ready to hear is _____

_____

4. Shape your family's beliefs and values

What values do I have about the situation that I want to share with my child?

_____

What beliefs are important for them to know?_____

_____

What do I not yet understand about my own beliefs and values?_____

_____

KEY POINTS FOR REFLECTION:

- Adults must research situations to know what information to share with children.
- Finding a support person or support people is essential for adults to feel emotionally safe and secure in this process.
- Determining what information a child is ready for and what information they are not ready for is part of the job as the adult in this conversation.
- Considering values and beliefs will help adults prepare for a child's questions and inform the messages they want to give the child.

9. INSTRUCTIONS II: THE CHANGES METHOD

Looping back around, as they say, let's return to the idea that we are all practicing these skills and that learning requires grace and patience. After an ankle injury sidelined my recreational running hobby, I decided to take up swimming lengths. How hard could swimming lengths be, really? I mean, I can play in the pool with my kids, I can keep myself afloat in the ocean, and I know how to splash around in the lake. I live on an island, for gosh sakes. Well,

The Courage to Communicate Model

Part One: Adult Pre Work

1. Do your research- Get informed
2. Find your people- Seek support
3. Cull the knowledge- Determine what to share
4. Shape your family's beliefs and values

Part Two: CHANGES Tool

Now you're here

5. The Communicating
C- Communicate what happened
H- How do you feel/What do you think?
A- And today...
N- Nerves, worries, and fears?
G- Going forward...
E- Everyone and everything that can help
S- Silly and serious questions

Part Three: Adult Post Work

6. Feel and release
7. Move forward

swimming lengths is actually incredibly hard and requires instruction, practice, and dedication. Stroke, stroke, breath, roll your hips to follow your shoulders, kick your feet, repeat. For me to learn the techniques and skills of swimming, I had to reach out to a professional for lessons. I needed a guide and the tools so I knew what and how to practice. It was intimidating to go into the pool for the first time as an adult asking for help about learning how to swim. There I was, awkwardly sitting on the bleachers beside the pool in my overly tight racer-back swimsuit, with a head condom on, and goggles putting so much suction on my face that it felt like I would have permanent indents around my eyes. Kids were wrapping up their swimming lessons, and wet little toddlers were walking past me to the change room. Don't be afraid of the nice lady, little babies. During the first few weeks, I had to fight off the panic I felt every time my head went under water. As a recovering control-seeking person, I sure didn't like the sensation of not being able to access air whenever I wanted. Putting ourselves in vulnerable situations where we are outside of our comfort zone brings a heightened awareness to all our "stuff." In my case, when I'm out of my depth (figuratively and literally in this case), I overthink, overanalyze, and desperately try to feel in control of some element of the situation.

Learning to swim lengths reminded me that letting go and trusting something or someone beyond yourself is just part of the learning experience. We struggle, we resist, and then, at some point, we surrender to the process and soar. If learning to communicate to your child about change is new for you, diving into Step 5 might feel a bit like sitting on those bleachers next to the pool. It doesn't have to be pretty, and it doesn't have to be bold, but I encourage you to dip a toe in. Trust the process, follow the guide, and practice.

If you have come this far in the process and you feel well-resourced to have this conversation without a communication tool, excellent! Chat away. While driving your child to soccer camp or washing their hair in the tub, you just focus your heart on their heart and pour out the information you have gathered. You are the expert on your situation, and there is no wrong way to do it. If you are a professional, you may have your own strategies you are comfortable using and that you find effective. There is no rule that you need to use a "tool" to share information. This is just one option offered to you. Please know you have my full permission to lovingly and compassionately speak with your child about the change they are going through without any specific tools, scripts, or workbooks. If, however, you want or need a tool, I've got one for you!

STEP 5: THE COMMUNICATING

Communication isn't just about speaking words. It's about hearing words, reading body language, feeling the other person's energetic response to your words, and knowing when to push forward and when to hold off. Having hard conversations like these can feel like walking on a frozen lake: each step tentative, every step scary. Are we going to make it to the other side, or are we going to step on a section of thin ice and crash through to the freezing water below? It can be frightening, and it absolutely takes practice.

One of the reasons I am able to say that empathic communication is my jam is because I feel my feelings in a really big way. Like, uncomfortably big. I feel all the feelings on the feeling spectrum. I have been described as "passionate" on more occasions than I care to count. When someone identifies for you that you sound passionate about a topic, it's a nice way of saying that you *feel intensity* about a topic. Often, that intensity is uncomfortable for people. It feels big, forceful, even scary. Sometimes that intensity is uncomfortable for me too, but most often, it just feels familiar. It's like my humanness can sometimes feel swallowed up by the darkness of my sadness. Like other moody creatives, I usually stand on the edge of a dark abyss anyway. I'm only one tiny push away from plunging headfirst into all the sadness in the world. I walk a fine line between funneling all my sensitivity into something creative and letting myself slip away into sadness and low-grade depression. I don't need any help feeling all my feelings, but sometimes I do need help knowing what to do with all those feelings. Do I cry, yell, scream, stomp? Do I hike, run, swim, bike? Do I hide, eat, and clean away those feelings? I do all those things, because sometimes it's all too much. That's the thing about being really good at feeling: sometimes you feel too much. Sometimes you feel all the feelings that aren't yours (yes, I know that this is what sends many people to therapy because this type of feeling can result in codependent and toxic relationships based on caretaking and emotional dependency, but that is also another book—thank goodness). In my case, I feel big and I feel dark and sometimes that means I express big, something that can be fairly uncomfortable for people too. Here's the gift all this "feeling" has given me: other people feeling big is perfectly normal to me. Watching someone feel all their feelings, even some of the most uncomfortable human emotions like grief and fear and shame and guilt, is okay for me. I can be present in that space with all those feelings and hold steady and continue the conversation, which means I continue to practice. If feeling and identifying those big feelings isn't something that feels like second nature to you, then it will be extra scary to approach these tough conversations with your kids. Initiating the conversation is like an invitation to feel and express, and that can be terrifying. If you are from a family where the norm was to lie, avoid, or deny feelings, inviting feelings to the party might seem unthinkable. Yet talking about the hard things is doing exactly that. Hello, uncomfortable feelings, let's bring you forward into the light because that's where we can talk about you. That's why this is scary. That's why talking about change and challenge is so frightening because it's talking about our feelings. And you know what talking about feelings leads to? It leads to *feeling* those feelings. And that, my friends, is how we limit compounding trauma and create opportunities to practice resilience. We talk, and we feel, and then we talk and feel some more. And then our good ol' friend Amy the Amygdala can go on more vacations when we are adults.

If you are at this step and you are feeling apprehensive, intimidated, or really uncomfortable, you are normal. It's difficult to talk about these things sometimes, and I'm not sure it gets easier with more living. Maybe the more tender the topic, the scarier it is to speak about. Talking about grief, loss, and broken hearts is still taboo for most of us. These topics are painful to speak about, and so we suffer in silence. Alone. Of course, we know that not talking about them doesn't protect any of us from having broken hearts, and it definitely doesn't help us heal from broken hearts. Yet we often turn away from painful things and unknowingly teach our children to turn away from them as well. If we don't tell children what they need to know about death and loss and help them find their own way through them, they will also suffer alone in silence. Even with my comfort level for big feelings, it's scary for me too. Even with my self-proclaimed skills for having hard conversations, I still wanted a tool to guide me through them. We have the CTCM to help us walk onto this frozen lake, and with one step at a time, we have these hard conversations in knowing that we must get across.

At this point in the process, you have done the research and you know what information you want to communicate. You have a support network for yourself, you've confirmed your message, and you've prepared for this conversation. It's *go* time. Do you still feel wildly lost on how to actually talk with your kids? That's okay. I've got you. The CHANGES tool offers a template for communicating that can be applied to any difficult change. It gives everyday parents, educators, and professionals like you and me a step-by-step guide that we can apply to our unique situation.

The CHANGES tool offers three steps for the adult to provide information and three steps for the child to provide information. Questions can be asked by both the adult and the child at any point, but also at the end of the process. The three steps for the adult to give information happen in sequence with the steps for the child to give information.

The CHANGES Communication Tool

C- Communicate what happened
Adult tells child what has occurred that has created a change in their life (emphasis is on the past)

H- How do you feel/what do you think?
Child tells adult what they think and feel about what has happened (emphasis is on the past)

A- And today...
Adult shares what is happening now (emphasis is on the present)

N- Nerves, worries, and fears?
Child tells adult what current worries and fears they have (emphasis is on the present)

G- Going forward...
Adult shares with child what might happen next (emphasis is on the future)

E- Everyone and everything that can help
Child shares with adult their perceived resources and supports (emphasis is on the future)

S- Silly and serious questions
Both child and adult can ask questions (emphasis is on the past, present, and future)

THE CHANGES COMMUNICATION TOOL

ADULT: C - Communicate What Happened (Past)

Here is where we put together all the tools we gathered. We bring forward the research, the information we culled, and our beliefs and values, and we tell our child what has happened. What change has occurred? We create space for our child to tell us how they feel about what has happened.

CHILD: H - How Do You Feel and What Thoughts Do You Have About What Happened? (Past)

This is where we want our child to tell us everything they think and feel about what happened. Remember how I mentioned that children make assumptions based on limited information? Here's where we hear all about those assumptions. We want them to get it all out, and it's our job to ask questions and illicit information so they can share. This isn't the time for us to share how we feel and what we think about this situation (because sadly, it's not about us even though it might actually be about us, but just not in this conversation), it is about intentionally asking questions to get the child to reflect on what they think and how these thoughts fuel their feelings.

ADULT: A - And Today . . . (Present)

And today, here is what is happening! Here is where we share what is happening now. This is the present moment. There may be some life situations that have been greatly affected by what happened, and this is where we lay those out for our child. Use words that keep your child in the present as much as possible during this step. "Right now," "in the moment," "for today," "this week," etc. Think about the small things that may be big things to your child. For example, changes to driving schedules, school attendance, family visits, or medical appointments.

CHILD: N - Nerves, Worries, and Fears. What worries and fears does the child have about what has happened in the past and what might happen in the future? (Present)

Take the lid off those worries and let them all pour out. Let your child's river of fear flow. This is where we really talk about being "in it," and there may be a lot swirling around. If you can get your child to brainstorm every possible scary thing that feels like it is happening, this is the place for it. Scary ideas lose a lot of their power when they get spoken out loud. Fear is only as big as our minds make it out to be. As your child downloads their worries and fears to you, embrace them without judgment or comment. Your only job here is to metaphorically hold those fears and worries in your heart and hands as your child lightens their load.

Note: Kids are amazing and they often find positives in the midst of the worst situations. This is also the step where you might hear about things they are excited about. They might like some of the changes and will want to talk about their happiness, hope, and joy in the middle of all the change. Let these positive ideas rain down on you like sprinkles on a sugar cookie. This is the sweet bite during a hard conversation. Welcome these ideas without judgment, just as you are welcoming all the other thoughts and feelings.

ADULT: G - Going Forward . . . What might happen next? (Future)

This is a really important step for us as adults to front-load our child with a picture of what the future *might* hold. Do we know how things will play out for sure? Likely not, but can we give them some idea of next steps? Yes. So, let's do it. To the best of your knowledge, let your child know how the next few weeks, months, years will look. Share the parts you do know and be clear about what you don't know. Telling your child that no one knows how something will go *is* actually telling them about the future and demonstrates to them that some things are in our control while other things are not. This may be where your beliefs and values are front and center, so be sure you didn't skip that step when you were prepping for this conversation.

CHILD: E - Everything and Everyone That Could Be Helpful: What resources and supports do we have going forward? (Future)

I told a friend recently that she already had all the resources she needed within herself to get through a difficult situation. It's a truth I know through lived experience. As adults, we are strong and capable humans who often need a reminder of our strength, especially when we can easily feel like victims of the things that happen to us. You know, eat the lemons, make the lemonade, plant the lemon seeds, etc. Or another classic expression, let it burn and then rise like the phoenix that you are. Maybe get that phoenix tattoo you always wanted while you're at it. We want to give children a version of this message too. We want them to start to see how they are strong and capable and resourceful, and that they can get through this difficult change because learning to thrive after hardship is a building block for resilience later in life. Their confidence is literally building one life struggle at a time, rather than being undermined or destroyed. Additionally, we also want to help children see the resources and supports that are available to them. We want to ask them what resources they have during this step. Imagine being informed about what your child's perception (which is your child's reality) of their supports are by having them tell you what they are?! Brilliant. Brilliant because when we know who and what brings them safety, support, and comfort, we know what to bring more of into their lives. We will also know where the gaps are and where we need to fill them. We need to know who their people are. Who they can talk to. What they can do when they are having a hard day. What things bring them comfort. Let your child tell you. They may be little, but they be mighty. By listening and creating space for *more* of whatever they need, we're giving our kids three messages: they are the experts on themselves, what feels safe and helpful to them matters to us, and we want to know what they need.

BOTH: S - Silly and Serious Questions

Anyone can ask questions during any of the above steps, but it's important to make time to see what questions have come up while working through the previous six steps. A curious mind is healthy and positive and something we want to nurture in our child. Many educators talk a lot about fostering a growth mindset in children. This means that they want their students to understand that everyone is capable of getting better at the skills they practice. Here we want our children to practice asking questions and making connections while ultimately expanding their understanding. We can show them that we are practicing our own growth mindset through this change as well by asking our own questions, seeking clarity from the child, and demonstrating that we are on our own learning journey as well.

Learning to swim lengths has felt pretty awkward for me. My body and mind are trying to coordinate, and it sure as sugar doesn't look pretty from the pool deck. But the more I practice, the more it comes together. I feel a little more confident every time I'm in the pool, and I have moments when it feels good, almost natural (there's no way around wearing that awful head condom though). I guess that's why people say the magic happens just outside your comfort zone. When you push yourself into a vulnerable and unfamiliar place, the potential to find a feeling of accomplishment and growth is exponential. This is hard work, and it takes big, bold bravery, but boy oh boy, I think the potential for positive outcomes is epic. Embrace the awkward, the unfamiliar, and the uncomfortable, and reach for the hope, the potential, and the resolve that communication can bring. And swim.

VANESSA'S EXPERIENCE . . .

Vanessa's story is a remarkable one of how empathic communication can be used to find connection, compassion, and healing. Her story begins with an overwhelming amount of sudden stress and change. While working hard to own and operate her own business, a busy preschool and childcare center, Vanessa was told by her husband of sixteen years that he was leaving her. While struggling to function and run her business through this devastating news, Vanessa kept facing new challenges. Within days, her husband (the one who just left her) was in an accident and broke multiple bones in his body, and her young son was diagnosed with a mysterious medical condition. While trying to take care of her injured husband and keep her business running successfully (she gives her staff a ton of credit for supporting her during this time), she also had to navigate taking her son for MRIs and to British Columbia's Children's Hospital for continued assessment. Vanessa writes:

So here I am. I feel as if my whole life is crashing in on me. My marriage is falling apart, my son has some strange lump in his leg that has doctors puzzled, and I'm hiding away from my business responsibilities and clients. I feel so helpless, as I have very little control over these situations. I have no idea how to navigate through something that feels so heavy yet still have it all together enough to care for not only my own children but also for the children in my center, plus run my business. I feel so much anguish, despair, guilt, blame, and depression.

And here is how Vanessa finds the strength and courage to move forward:

On one particular morning, most of the children in my preschool seemed to be more emotional than usual, unwilling to problem solve or resolve conflicts, and just having a hard time in general. It was at that very moment that something clicked for me. Prior to my own recent adversities, I had guided young children and supported them in developing crucial life skills such as emotional regulation, problem solving, conflict resolution, focus and self-control, communication, critical thinking, making connections, and so many more. How could I expect to teach these skills when I was merely "juggling" or "making it work?" If I truly wanted to make a difference and make positive impacts, I needed to look within myself, accept this change, and practice the very skills that I teach every day. I needed to model them myself. I needed to communicate and connect. That day, at circle time, I told my students that I noticed most of them were having a hard morning. I then shared with my students that I had been having a hard time lately as well (I spared a lot of the detail, but my emotions were 100 percent genuine). I told them I had big worries and that I had very big feelings (anger, sadness, etc.). My students saw me cry as I was explaining to them that it can be very hard to deal with things that we feel we have no control over in our lives. I felt so touched when they started to share their worries and stories such as when their pets or grandparents passed away, when they lost their favorite toy, and when they fought with their siblings. Almost every single child had something "hard" to share, and they shared their stories with such powerful emotions behind them. I felt heard and connected with, and so did they. We practiced deep breathing and spoke of the things we were grateful for despite our hardships. From that moment on, I found great strength in my vulnerability. I had a new sense of confidence in "not having control" over situations. Instead, I have control over how I choose to react to them, and I don't let negative situations determine or change my character in the process. In almost every behavior intervention workshop or course I have done over the years, they talk about the direct relation between children's behaviors and the type of connections/attachments they have in their lives. Therefore, we as childcare providers do our very best to make sure these children feel a sense of security and connection with us. What better way to achieve this then to truly connect by sharing our own vulnerabilities and experiences, and to model the resiliency that we teach.

A year out from this difficult time, Vanessa shares what she learned:

I learned a lot about myself in this period of my life (and I am still learning, of course), and I am still on a journey of discovery and growth. However, I don't feel so heavy and helpless. As a matter of fact, I feel more connected and in tune with myself than I ever have. I ended up closing my preschool center to focus more of my attention on my family, and I am now working for an agency that focuses on supporting young children with diverse needs. I feel extremely proud and blessed to be able to continue to support, guide, and care for children in their group environments. Although we are still faced with our ups and downs and are still dealing with the hurt of it all, my husband and I have grown stronger together. We are and still choose to be each other's best friend every day. My son's "bump" is still a bit of a mystery, and it is still a stressful situation, but steps are being taken and appointments are booked to ensure that he has the care he needs. We will face this together as a family.

I have learned that in the face of adversity, maintaining healthy attachments, strong connections, and open communication (with genuine emotions) with our children or the children we care for is key. It is important to remember that not only do children need to feel safe and secure, but we as caregivers and parents do as well.

Maintaining routines, self-care, positive self-views, communication, and a positive perspective are all critical in building and modeling resilience and coping skills. Moving toward goals (small or big), helping others or asking for help, accepting change while staying true to ourselves, forming connections, and taking breaks when needed is not always easy to do in today's world and while facing difficult situations, but it is through these actions and mindsets that we teach our children (and ourselves) what we are made of and how to find the courage within ourselves.

Vanessa is a wife, mother, and Early Childhood Educator in the Central Vancouver Island area. Her gift for connection is felt by all the families whose lives she touches. Vanessa continues to swap out surviving for thriving and reaches for the healthiest, happiest life possible.

YOUR EXPERIENCE ...

Practice telling your child what has happened by completing the C step in the CHANGES Communication Tool: I would tell my child _____

_____

Prepare some questions you would like to ask your child by completing the S step in the CHANGES Communication Tool: Two questions I have for my child are _____

_____

KEY POINTS FOR REFLECTION:

- Communicating with children about change involves an adult telling a child what happened in the past, what is happening now, and what might happen in the future.

- Asking children what they feel and think is part of this process.

- Finding out what worries and fears a child might have will help adults understand the child's experience.

- Determining how a child perceives their support helps adults know how to increase and enhance their resources.

10. INSTRUCTIONS III: THE ADULT POST WORK

In the Adult Pre Work, we took steps to prepare and regulate ourselves for communicating. In the final steps in the Adult Post Work, we take action to continue that regulation for ourselves, to create opportunities for our children to regulate themselves, and for the two of us (or more!) to be co-regulated. A reminder that co-regulation is when we share the calm in our bodies and minds to bring calm to our children's bodies and minds (this reminder is mostly for my husband, who I sincerely hope is still reading this book).

The Courage to Communicate Model

Part One: Adult Pre Work

1. Do your research- Get informed
2. Find your people- Seek support
3. Cull the knowledge- Determine what to share
4. Shape your family's beliefs and values

Part Two: CHANGES Tool

5. **The Communicating**

C- Communicate what happened
H- How do you feel/What do you think?
A- And today...
N- Nerves, worries, and fears?
G- Going forward...
E- Everyone and everything that can help
S- Silly and serious questions

Part Three: Adult Post Work

6. Feel and release
7. Move forward

Finally, you're here

Dr. Vanessa Lapointe, a child psychologist, has dedicated her career to help-ing parents "grow themselves up" while they "grow up" their children.[41] She teaches how connected and informed parenting can look, cheers for "big people" everywhere to parent compassionately, and provides parents with ways they can attune and regulate to their children to best solve problems, comfort, correct, and guide.[42] She offers a motto to parents that prompts them to see their child's behavior, feel what is going on for them, and be what the child needs. Her "See It, Feel It, Be It" mantra shows parents that they don't necessarily need specific tools or skills to learn how to be present for their children, but rather to trust their intuition and be available with compassion and connection. If this idea sounds good to you but you have no idea to achieve it, the CTCM is here for you. The steps in the CTCM help us live Dr. Lapointe's motto by giving us a recipe to see what our children are going through, to feel what it is like for them by listening and asking questions, and to show up for them by being present, doing the work with them, celebrating, and moving forward. By completing Steps 1–5 of the CTCM, we've done most of the work; we just have the final two steps left to complete. If we were in the kitchen making seven dozen cookies, we would have five batches cooling on the counter and two dozen left to pop in the oven. Keep scooping because these last two dozen are just as sweet.

STEP 6: FEEL AND RELEASE

The word combination of "feel and release" might sound touchy-feely or woo-woo for you, and I get that. They feel that way to me too. Ignore that inclination and read on, because this step is an important acknowledgment of how hard communicating can be. What you have just done *was* hard. Your mind, heart, and body have likely put a ton of energy and emotion into this process, and now there will be a release. Potentially a collapse. Depending on how hard "the work" was, there is a need for everyone involved to physically release the intensity that gets built up during difficult conversations. After we have these conversations, after we do this work, this step gives us permission to take the space to feel the relief and to let go of all the intensity. If communicating is the "heavy lift," then feeling and releasing is the "easy lift." Acknowledge the effort, regardless of the outcome. Pause to accept the job well done.

STEP 7: MOVING FORWARD

Now we move forward. But what does "forward" look like? We often don't know, and that's okay. As the change evolves and our children grow and expand developmentally, the next steps will tumble forward on their own. New questions may be asked. New fears and worries might be brought forward by your child, and so we go back to researching, culling, shaping beliefs, and sharing information. But for now, the work is done. We need to let our children know that we have completed the process for the time being and that we can return to it again when and if we need to. I liken this final step to using a period in writing. Grammar rules tell us that punctuation (like periods) tell us when to pause to breathe. It doesn't mean the paragraph won't continue, but the sentence is over and it's time to take a break. Use this step to help your child take a break from the work of processing and understanding change in any way that feels right for you. Do whatever feels right to ensure you can put a period behind all the hard work you and your child have done. Pause. Breathe. Move forward.

Scrape the sides of the mixing bowl, toss it in the sink, and grab a warm cookie, because you deserve it! You've completed the CTCM process from Step 1 to Step 7, and that's no easy bake, but before we start to clean the kitchen, let's look at how the CTCM can actually be used in real life. Let's look at how change plays out. Let's put the cookie metaphors to the side, although it pains me to do so, and get real, real. To kick off the getting real, Talia shares her recent experience of change and how different the communication through those changes can be with adults and children.

TALIA'S EXPERIENCE . . .

When I think back on the last three years that were so full of change and challenge, I wonder what my kids will say when they are grown and we are reflecting back on this time. I can picture us all around the supper table with memories being shared, but the discussion that comes next is so hard to imagine.

How will they tell the story of learning that Mom had cancer? Or watching me navigate the pain and challenges I experienced afterward? Or about the separation of their father and me? Or how I told them that I was gay?

I felt so much worry about getting it wrong. Sharing too much with them, the wrong thing. Forcing them from their innocence and into the possibility of worry or future therapy. I would read for hours on how to tell kids things. Pour over websites, second-guess myself, and generally worry that I would completely fuck them up.

Telling adults was so different. When you tell a grown-up about a major event, you know you're going to get some kind of a reaction. Sometimes a predictable one. I knew my parents would not handle my cancer diagnosis well. I was right. I knew that the hardest person to tell I was queer would be one of my dearest friends who just wants the world to always make sense and be neat and tidy. And I knew my dad, who deeply cares for my ex, would not understand my need to end the relationship.

I knew these challenges would come because of their own experiences and filters. They took in my information, then swirled it through their own life's understanding, trying to make sense of it through their worldview. Some of their histories I knew, and some I discovered as I shared. I had to navigate their reactions: the intensity of knowing I probably wasn't going to die but their absolute terror in hearing the "C" word and their worst-case scenario thoughts; picturing loved ones they had lost; a friend disappearing for a year, later stating that my diagnosis sent her reeling with unresolved feelings after losing her mother to cancer; folks seeing the scar on my neck, then having their insecurities about their own imperfections coming up, challenging the idea of showing mine so visibly; hearing about their parents' divorces when I shared that my marriage was over, or telling me that they had a spouse cheat on them and wondering if I had a secret lover too. And coming out . . . Well, fortunately, I mostly received love and very little surprise, but I did hear stories of queer aunties, saw knowing looks, and even heard secrets of their own experiments with girls in a corner of a bar.

But with the kids, there was just this absolutely different experience. What in their lives could possibly prepare them? What would their understanding be rooted in? I offered them the diagnosis framed within the certainties I knew. It was treatable. There would be surgery. The doctors were really good at their jobs. It would be challenging. We would do our best to keep things as normal as we could. Life would change and then be okay again eventually.

Okay, they said.
Will you die? No.
Okay.

Later check-ins would tell me that there were worries I never expected or could have prepared for: like my daughter who thought that I would have a hole in my neck, gaping open forever, or questioning why I ended up in significant chronic pain from the surgeries and wasn't getting better like I said I would. So, we would talk and clarify, and I learned to ask more questions. I also explained that we can't predict the future, no matter how much we want to.

I strategized how to tell them my marriage to their father was ending but also reassure them that our love for them was unchanged and that we would do our best to keep their lives as normal as possible. I set the tone for where and how this discussion would take place. We drove to the beach to have a safe, undistracting space. We welcomed their thoughts and worries. And there were a few tears. Then, weeks later, I navigated a very big question from my eldest on whether my love would change for him since it had changed for his dad. My heart hurt over the way he was trying to figure everything out, and I couldn't speak quickly enough to say how different it was and how impossible it was to stop loving him.

Telling my kids that I am queer was the scariest topic in some ways. I worried more that their friends would tease them or that they would have to experience the homophobia I know still exists in the world. Or that they wouldn't understand. My daughter was thrilled. The world needs more lesbians, Mom! My son, in his quiet way, said he loved me. And then later we discussed how being true to ourselves was the most important thing of all. He asked how I knew, how I was sure, and how I felt. He had genuine curiosity and appreciation for this new information.

What I noticed most in sharing with them is how it became a part of my own growth through each of these challenges and the realization that I am creating their future worldview. I found motivation for rehab after my surgeries in wanting to play and engage with them. And I could speak to them about pain and disability and learning when to rest and when to push myself.

I wanted to end my marriage for so many reasons but also show them that we are allowed to change and grow and need more, to not settle, and that we deserve happiness and joy. So, as we talked about separation and the loss and grieving, we also discussed why it's okay.

I couldn't pretend my queerness didn't matter once I wondered what kind of example I was setting by shutting my own truth away. And when I shared it with them, I spoke about how full of joy I was to live my life free and open. Acknowledging it was still hard and scary to do, and I kept the inner workings from them until I could speak from a place of clarity so that I could speak to the uncertainty with a different voice—from "parent" me, not "worried me" who was navigating all of it.

We are in this together. I will continue to be safe and solid and parent you. My process is ongoing, but I am an adult, and I will take care of myself.

You will be the child. You will watch me grow, and you will have questions and moments of not understanding, but together, these changes will also help you learn to navigate your own life.

You are not sheltered from the realities of life, but you are not expected to fix me or help me or own any of this.

We are together in this as a family, but I am responsible for me.

So again, as I picture us at the table, reminiscing about these times that I wanted to be over and through and part of history, I truly wonder what they will say. Maybe that we carry on as bravely as we can, and that when we are rooted in love and intention, it will be just fine. Or maybe I should start saving for their therapy bills. Probably both.

Talia. Badass creative, kitchen goddess, and mom, bravely living life on British Columbia's wild west coast. You can find her on IG @talia_beltgens

YOUR EXPERIENCE . . .

Two of the ways I like to celebrate completing hard work are _____

_____

My favorite activity to release built-up energy, stress, and tension is _____

_____

One of the ways my child likes to celebrate is by _____

_____

KEY POINTS FOR REFLECTION:

- Acknowledging the completion of this work is part of the process.
- Releasing the experience and celebrating can be done in multiple ways prior to moving forward.
- Although change is often ongoing, the CTCM invites children to acknowledge the completion of, and to move forward from, this work.

11. METHODOLOGY AND IMPLEMENTATION I: THE ADULT PRE WORK

It's great to have instructions, but sometimes we need to know how those instructions can play out in real life. When I look at new cookie recipes, often the reviews and comments are just as helpful as the ingredient list. Reading ideas about how the recipe could be used not only helps me feel like it's an achievable task (like, I'm actually going to get a delicious product), but it also helps me feel connected to other bakers. When I use the words methodology and

---

The Courage to Communicate Model

Part One: Adult Pre Work

1. Do your research- Get informed
2. Find your people- Seek support
3. Cull the knowledge- Determine what to share
4. Shape your family's beliefs and values

Part Two: CHANGES Tool

5. **The Communicating**
C- Communicate what happened
H- How do you feel/What do you think?
A- And today...
N- Nerves, worries, and fears?
G- Going forward...
E- Everyone and everything that can help
S- Silly and serious questions

Part Three: Adult Post Work

6. Feel and release
7. Move forward

We've here again

implementation, I'm intending to offer ideas about how this recipe could be used for parents, educators, and therapists. These are just ideas, and like anything else, take what helps and leave what doesn't. Nuts in cookies aren't for everyone, so omit as necessary. Additionally, while we talk about how these steps could be used in real life, let's talk about change *in real life*. Let's take a look at this story from a childcare provider who owned and operated her own facility at the time the COVID-19 global pandemic hit.

KYM'S EXPERIENCE . . .

The day started just like any other: the sun was shining as I woke up and rushed off to work, basically the moment my eyes were open. The rush to work was the same; greeting the children at school was the same; the roller coaster of our everyday schedule complete with laughter, tears, and general chaos was the same. I work with children who are between the ages of eighteen months and five years; we like to keep things the same. And on this particular day, everything, within reason, was the same . . . until our quiet time.

As the children were resting, I was finally able to focus on the texts I was getting.

What are my plans?
Will I be staying open?
Should they come get their children right now?

I looked at the news. COVID was here (something in my ignorance I had heard nothing about previously). People were getting sick, people were dying, and the virus seemed to be everywhere: businesses, schools, centers—everything was closing. The reality of the situation seemed overwhelmingly scary. My brain went into high alert, trying to logically process all the information in front of me. I reassured my families that I would be monitoring the situation, that I was unlikely to close unless ordered to, but that they were welcome to do what they felt was best for themselves and their children.

By the next day, as we celebrated our St. Patrick's Day party, I had three of my regular eight children in attendance. Although I tried to make the day as normal as possible for them, it very obviously wasn't. I still remember attempting to take the usual cheery photo of them dressed up at our green-themed snack but being met with uncharacteristic silence. This was probably the moment my heart broke. I could deal with my stress and all the questions, fear, frustration, and even anger coming at me from the media and adults I knew, but when it affected the children and took their joy, wonder, and awe away, I knew something had to change.

As the next few days went by, the situation continuously changed. All of society seemed to shut down. I went on my planned spring break, but I was full of stress about how I was going to survive financially in the broken system of childcare, being self-employed, and counting on a significant group of paying families in my care to make any kind of living wage. I also felt shame and regret that they would be stuck with a bill they wouldn't even make use of for months at a time. I was in constant communication with families, trying to figure out what we were all going to do for the long run, and all in all, no one knew what they were going to do. Finally, government funding programs such as the Temporary Emergency Fund were introduced to encourage childcare centers to stay open, and a weight was definitely lifted, but it was by far not the only weight.

The questions about and pressure of the changing times continued to develop, and by the time I went back to work, I only had two children: a sibling group consisting of a child who regularly attended and a child who had long ago moved on from my care. Occasionally, I also had one or two other children. By that time, the children knew that their friends were staying home because of the virus, and they had formed their own reasoning as to why, but I had no idea what their thoughts were. As a teacher, I really like throwing them a good "well, why do you think that is" question, so I asked them. The way they saw it, the virus could be anywhere, and we weren't safe until we could get a vaccine that would kill it. That statement right there was huge! Now, from my side, I could see exactly how they worked out that conclusion. In fact, many adults seemed to have the same thought, and it seemed like a very simple "child appropriate" way to put it, but I also knew that the reality of the situation was much more complex, and this simple statement left a lot of room for fear, uncertainty, and disappointment further down the road. I could hear their fear over leaving the safety of home to go to a different environment with different people. I knew that, as their teacher, I needed to assure them that I had their safety in mind even when they weren't home and in the safety of their parents' arms. Luckily, I had a relationship with these children, and that relationship meant that we had trust—trust that I refused to shatter with simple, misleading information.

And this is exactly the moment where the CTCM could be applied.

(Kym's story continues a bit later in this chapter.)

STEP 1 IN ACTION: DO YOUR RESEARCH

Due to the universal experience of difficult life changes, the world is full of content on just about any topic you want to research. Start a binder with resources you find or create a drawer in your office where you compile info sheets and things you want to remember. You may wish to keep notes on your phone. Take photos of handouts, screenshot the website of a professional that is recommended to you, text yourself something to follow up on. Or don't. You can follow the breadcrumbs others leave for you and keep moving forward gathering more information for yourself and that fits for your family as you go. You can keep a mental list or a cluster of facts near and dear to your heart. There is no right or wrong way to gather information; the point is that you are taking action. With every action you take to find out more about the particular change your child is experiencing, the more you will feel like taking action. One step will lead to another. Here are a few questions to help you start digging for helpful and accurate information:

- What do I need to know about this topic to feel confident in talking about it?
- What books on this topic are available?
- What reputable websites specialize in it?
- Who is talking about it on social media?
- Who hosts podcasts on this topic?
- Does my local government or health authority provide information I need to know?
- Who are the informed experts who will have the most current information? (Think lawyers, realtors, doctors, community leaders, hospice workers, disaster response professionals, etc.)
- What information do I need to get in writing?

FOR THE EDUCATORS

It's my impression that teachers are often expected to keep their students feeling safe and secure in the world without being provided with the necessary information. If you work in a school setting, there are hierarchical-type systems in place, and information only trickles down on occasion. I also suspect that you may hear lots of bits and pieces from children about the changes they are going through, but you may have little to no contact with an adult to confirm or clarify what you are hearing. Whether addressing a change with a group of students or an individual student, the best approach, given the limited options, may be to use this step as a "to-do" step with your students. Instead of being the adult who does all the research so that you can facilitate this conversation, you can say to your students, "The first step here is for us to get informed. What do we need to know about what is happening? What do we already know and what do we need to know more of? How do we find out what we need to know? Who do we trust to ask?" I know you already ask these types of questions when teaching curriculum. You use these strategies all the time to ensure your students learn the content you want to teach them. You can apply any pedagogy (look at me using teacher jargon!) you feel comfortable with to teach the Adult Pre Work in the CTCM, consequently creating *Student* Pre Work. For example, some educators could choose to use a concept-based instruction approach to help their students link their lived experiences to the "big ideas" of each CTCM step. Just as you would use teaching strategies and methodologies to teach your students theories and concepts in the topic areas of science or social studies, you can apply those same tools to addressing your students' social-emotional needs by offering them opportunities to become *detectives of knowledge*. I may not be a classroom teacher, but I know that teaching students the skills of putting on their detective hats, asking questions, and looking for answers creates adults who have the know-how to do the same when they need answers the most. As they say, it is all about creating lifelong learners (they say that, right?!).

FOR THE THERAPISTS

As a caring professional who has perhaps been tasked with working with a child or children to talk to them about a difficult change, you are likely trying to get information from the parents or the referral source (social worker, doctor, or similar). I can only imagine how tricky it is to get the whole story when you are missing a few or more puzzle pieces! You also don't need a book written by me to tell you that the more information you can gather about someone's situation prior to working with them, the better. My hope is that this step clarifies that having an opportunity to be informed is in actuality essential to the work you are about to do. Telling parents or a referring adult that you need to have information shared with you about a medical diagnosis, a parental separation situation, a family's loss, a move, or a local tragedy is essential to the outcome of your work with a child or a family.

For example, if a child and family therapist is asked to work with a child about the ongoing pandemic due to concerns that it has affected the child's mental health, the therapist needs to be informed about how the pandemic has affected the family: How did they address masks, vaccines, isolation, and/or school attendance? Understanding how the pandemic *hit* the family over the last couple of years and the day-to-day is an absolute must. Using this example, some questions may be:

- Did your work or career have to change during the pandemic?
- Was your child unable to continue contact with extended family or other loved ones?
- How has your stress been during the last two years?
- Did you have to move during the pandemic?

I know it sounds obvious, but how often as therapeutic professionals are we prompted to ask questions specific only to the child without having the permission to ask "data-collection" questions that are needed to support a child from an informed place? Think about presession information gathering that asks parents questions like: "How has this change affected your sleep and the night-time sleep of other family members?" rather than one like: "How is your child sleeping?" You may still be consulting your bookshelf, or a colleague who specializes in a topic to complete the research you need, but you also absolutely will need to gather research from the adults in the family to see a full picture of the child's situation.

STEP 2 IN ACTION: FIND YOUR PEOPLE

The truth is, there is going to be a lot to process and talk about, and our kids aren't the people for doing that. Kids can't be our sounding boards. When we want to swear, yell, and shake our fists at the sky (because many of life's changes are unfair), we need another adult to hold that space for us. We need a safe person to hold our thoughts, fears, anger, and sadness away from our child, because we are going to be *that* place for our child. We are the safe "cookie jar" for our child's big feelings. I'm not suggesting that we aren't learning and processing with our children, but I am suggesting that we first need to do our own work with a trusted person so that we can choose what we process with our children. If we don't do our own work, we will inadvertently end up working out our stuff on our children. They deserve for us to show up for them as supported and strong adults, as sure as possible of the facts and figures of the situation. They get to be messy and afraid and fall apart all over us, while we hold steady with strong arms and big, big shoulders.

Picture yourself showing your child that you go for a walk with Aunty Jenny every other week so that you can talk about how you feel. You walk, you talk, you process, and then you carry on doing. We cannot expect our little people to share and grow with us if we aren't also sharing and growing with another safe human.

Questions to ask yourself when considering who your people are and how you might find them:
- What support groups did I come across when I was searching for research on social media platforms and the internet?
- Who do I know that has been through something similar? Do I like how they handled it? Can I relate to them?
- Is paying for a professional support person an option for me? Where could I ask for a recommendation for a great professional?
- Who in my current friend and family circle feels safest to me? Who do I trust the most?

- Who in my friend and family circle do I not trust?
- If my car broke down on the highway in the middle of the night, who would I call?
- If I had to share my favorite cookies with someone in my life, who would it be?
- Who do I already know that really likes my kids?
- Do I like being supported by a group of people or do I like having one close support?

Do some soul searching and see who in your life could be your support person. You may also wish to consider who isn't that person for you. A difficult life change often shifts our group of friends or close family members. You might be surprised who rises to support you, and you might be surprised who doesn't.

FOR THE EDUCATORS

Once you secure your own people, your task is in assisting your student detectives to determine who their people are. Can they give some examples of their support people and how they make an impact on your life? Depending on the grade level you teach, you may wish to do some mind mapping and brainstorming with your class. Or tag it into a writing assignment. There are a lot of different ways this step could be tied to the curriculum, so do whatever you need to do to target multiple teaching goals. And if you have a student who can't identify even one support person in their life, your community of learners needs to go to work to solve that problem. No one gets left behind.

FOR THE THERAPISTS

Providing therapeutic interventions can be isolating work, and most training programs drill into their students' heads that in order to maintain a healthy counseling practice, therapists need a support network. They need clinical supervision and colleagues they can lean on and brainstorm with as they support individuals through difficult life situations. The career of "therapy" instills in its employees that a support network is a requirement of the job, so assuming that you have one in place for yourself, your role here is to walk a family or child through this step. What this step really prompts a professional to do is to explore what support looks like, sounds like, and feels like for a family. If a child or adult has never had a healthy support person, it may take some intentional guiding. This isn't a box to tick, it is a step in the process of therapeutic intervention.

STEP 3 IN ACTION: CULL THE INFORMATION

When we start to dig through the information we have and determine what we want to tell our children, we are truly focusing on their needs. It is all about what would be helpful for them to know at this time in their lives, taking into consideration age, stage, and cognitive abilities. It is helpful to consider what assumptions they may have that you'll need to address or what false facts they may have heard. Think about what you already know about how your child thinks and be ready with information that will address their questions and concerns. Really let your imagination go wild here and think about how confusing life was when you were young. Think about all the things you misunderstood about the world when you were in elementary school. I guarantee your child has a handful of misunderstandings already dancing in their mind and heart, and they need you to bring them hard facts, clarity, and the straight goods. Be ready with those "off the list" things now so that when your child asks you directly, you can respond with a calm and loving statement of affirmation: "That's a really important question, and I can understand why you would ask that" or "Some details about what is happening are for just the adults to know about. What I can tell you is . . ."

You may need to start with a crash course in your child's developmental age and stage to help you determine what's appropriate for them. Our kids change so rapidly that it's hard to keep up with them, so a quick internet search of developmental stages should help inform you. It is also helpful to have this information fresh in our minds in case we need to remind other loved ones that our child's abilities are limited by their age and stage. Sometimes, with the best of intentions, we expect more from our children than is possible based on their brain development. Remember that our children do not have the same skills we do when it comes to decision-making, memory, understanding, impulse control, and overall functioning. We also need to be mindful of children with exceptional differences that impact maturity. Your child's chronological age may not match their social and emotional age, which is an important factor when determining what to share. Some questions to ask yourself that might help you get clarity on what information to cull from all the knowledge you now have are:

- What does my child need to know to feel safe and secure in this situation?
- What information might increase my child's worries and fears?
- What information do I want to save to share in a few years?
- How can I provide my child with information in a way they will understand?
- If I could only tell my child three things about this change, what would they be?
- What information can I give that will prevent my child from making assumptions about this situation?

- What information will create the least amount of confusion?

FOR THE EDUCATORS

Isn't this what you do so well for a living? You teach content to specific ages and stages at a level they understand, right? Teachers constantly shift and modify their lesson plans to accommodate the different learning levels and needs in their classes so that their content continues to be appropriate as their class demographics change. So, basically, you do this every day. Shifting information so that it fits the audience is your specialty, and you need no further explanation from me on how to do it. The only variable in this situation is that you are now teaching your students how to cull their own information. Depending on the developmental stage you teach, you're likely already doing it. Think about how you support children to share something at circle time that is relevant to the class. Or how you get your students to read a newspaper article and then tell you the important parts. Or if you teach older students, you may be working with your class to prepare science projects that give the audience the needed information to understand the experiment. These are all examples of culling the information with their new knowledge. This step gives your students the opportunity to transfer those skills to the life experience or the difficult change you are mentoring them to work through.

FOR THE THERAPISTS

What at first looked like working with a child to understand a change is starting to look very much like working with parents, right? That's the thing about the Adult Pre and Post Work: working with the parents is part of the therapeutic work, and it requires just as much time and attention as talking to the child about what they are going through. Ultimately, working with children is working with families, and therapy is designed to be a short-term intervention for a child. We want to support the family unit to go forward positively without us, so we insert ourselves into people's lives briefly, provide intervention, and then back out, leaving the family stronger than when we met them. It's an ideal, I know.

STEP 4 IN ACTION: SHAPE YOUR FAMILY'S BELIEFS AND VALUES

Determining our own beliefs and values in preparation for talking to our children might seem simple at first, but it's actually going to be quite heavy. Considering our personal values and beliefs about loss, life, and love are not things we usually talk about over coffee with friends or around the dinner table with our parents. Sometimes, as adults, we haven't been given an opportunity to consider what we believe and why we believe it. It can require a deep dive into ourselves, and that can be uncomfortable, but if we don't do this step, we won't be ready for the questions our children may ask. You know that question that most adults stumble with and around for most of their lives? The "why do bad things happen" one? It is often at the core of our children's questions when things are difficult. We don't have to have the answer, but we need to have clarity on what our beliefs and values are so we can support our kids to make sense of this confusing life experience. When a child has to deal with a loss, it is almost always unfair, unjust, and illogical. When we look for answers to our children's questions, regardless of what we believe about pain and trauma, confirming that the pain they experience is not their fault is a priority. As you shape your beliefs and struggle to explain the unexplainable, you are helping them to shape their own beliefs.

Questions that you can ask yourself to help you determine your values and beliefs in preparation for the hard questions your child might ask are:

- Do I believe that someone is at fault in this situation?
- Do I believe that everything happens for a reason?
- Do I believe a higher power has a plan for me?
- Do I believe when one door closes another opens?
- Do I believe that God never gives me more than I can handle?
- What am I going to say if my child asks me why bad things happen?
- What do I think about the idea of karma?
- Why do I feel that it is important to talk about this topic?
- What are my values about my child's experience?

FOR THE EDUCATORS

I listen to my kids tell me the questions their teachers get asked, and I shudder a little inside. When children are in their primary years, teachers seem to be the go-to people for all of life's important questions. They're the type of life questions parents don't want to answer. Teachers have to be inclusive and careful when answering these big questions, because they are walking a fine line of not offending a family by giving the impression they are imposing their personal values and beliefs on someone else's child. It is difficult to be the go-to person for children asking hard questions. I suggest that this step be approached from the angle of offering your students an awareness that beliefs and values are something we can all craft. Maybe you'll be the first person to explain to your students what values and beliefs are, how they come to be part of who we are, and how we can change them as we grow up. Like literacy and numeracy, understanding beliefs and values is an important part of the social-emotional wellness for children. This step is an essential part of the curriculum.

FOR THE THERAPISTS

It takes a unique skill set to help a family shape their own beliefs, and I can assure you it is a specific type of therapeutic work that doesn't happen that often. We tend to talk about our values and beliefs when we are getting married (I love him; I'm so happy we have similar values) and divorced (I can't stand him; it turns out we have very different values), but we don't often pause to check in on our values during a major life change. While in the midst of change, it's a prime time to put our values and beliefs at the forefront of our minds. It's an ideal time to help parents, or a family, work through what values they have in common, what doesn't fit for them anymore, and what they would like to shift going forward. Like some of the other steps, this is specific and dedicated work that can be facilitated with the help of a professional.

As Kym's story continues, she shares how she gave the children in her care information and created safety and security for them, intuitively using an approach similar to the Courage to Communicate Model.

KYM'S EXPERIENCE CONTINUES . . .

I spent the next couple weeks teaching them safety precautions such as cleaning, washing hands, physical distancing, etc., as well as the reasoning behind those safety precautions. We talked about germs in general (both good and bad), how the body and its immune system functions, and how vaccines work. I wanted them to have a really good grasp on how their body and their world works in order to reduce the fear that every germ is bad and that they can appear out of nowhere, while also preparing them for the soon-to-be-shattered idea that a vaccine will miraculously save the world by killing the virus and thus allowing the world to continue on as it once was.

We still spoke in simple, developmentally appropriate, and relatable ways, and we allowed room for different personal values/beliefs, but we grounded our conversations in facts and reality. We talked about what the virus basically was (germs), why this virus was so different from every other germ they hear about (i.e., a brand-new baby germ that no one knew about that was really dangerous for some), and how our bodies have ninja fighters (white blood cells) that fight the bad germs and protect us. We went into detail about how the ninja fighters couldn't fight if they didn't know what the bad germs looked like, and because the virus was just a baby virus, no ninja fighter knew what it looked like. We went on to connect how the vaccine (that scientists were working on) would help ninja fighters know what to look for so they can fight before the bad germs overrun them, but that the virus would always be here, we would just know how to fight it better and wouldn't get so sick. We connected as much as we could so that it all made sense to them. The conversations were amazing. The children seemed so relieved to hear that the situation was not as scary as they had imagined; that they had a full support system complete with parents, teachers, and scientists all working on the problem; and that their own body was not as helpless as it originally seemed. I always tell them that our bodies are amazing things, but now they could really see why. And better yet, their imaginations were working with realistic information that made the threat much more manageable.

Now, more than two years later, I am still helping children cope with this pandemic. I am still under an immense amount of pressure from the world around me as I struggle, often feeling unsupported, in a society divided and torn in almost every conceivable perspective possible. Looking at the simple explanation I provided for the children, I am sure many would rip it apart as a fictional misrepresentation of reality strictly because of their own misaligned beliefs and/or the language we used to relate abstract ideas for young children. It is my belief that, with my own worries, concerns, and beliefs aside, children are learning how they work together with the world. They may not quite understand all our worries, the language we hear/use around those worries, or how everything is connected, but they absolutely worry (especially about what unseen/scary things we silently worry about in times of change). When this happens, it is usually time to put aside our concerns, beliefs, and biases to really connect with them and hear their questions and worries, all while grounding in the reality of factual information provided to them in a way that they will understand. I say the same thing to families coping with death, divorce, or any other big change. It can be so hard to put your own beliefs and emotions aside, and while acknowledging everyone's feelings, really look logically at the changes/worries. They don't need to know all the ins and outs of how this situation came to be or what it means, but they do need to be able to make sense of the world, what it means for them, how we can respectfully take care of ourselves and those around us, and that they are safe, so if that means that we are going to discuss how white blood cells are like the tiny ninja fighters of our body, that is what we'll do, because they know ninja fighters, and I know they're safe.

Born and raised on Vancouver Island, Kym has always had a passion for working with children and being what they need when they need it. She has been learning, building, and growing in the childcare field for more than ten years and continues to aspire to make a difference in the world and the little minds that will become our world. Although our lives are constantly under intense pressure, Kym believes children deserve the best future we can offer, and she strives daily to meet this challenge with courage, honesty, patience, and integrity.

YOUR EXPERIENCE . . .

What is one action step you can take today to:

Find a needed piece of information? _____

_____

Connect with someone who cares about you? _____

_____

Learn about your child's developmental stage (their chronological age and/ or their maturity level)? _____

_____

Ask a trusted support person what values they see you having in this situation? Does what they offer fit for you? Does it not fit? _____

_____

KEY POINTS FOR REFLECTION:

- As parents, educators, and therapists, there are different ways to achieve each step.
- There are many different ways to move forward and take action.
- The act of doing one step will create forward momentum during the Adult Pre Work, making it easier to complete other steps.

12. METHODOLOGY AND IMPLEMENTATION II: THE CHANGES TOOL IN ACTION

Talking about why we want or need to do something is fairly easy. Writing about why it's important and why it matters is also fairly easy. Talking about *how* we actually do the "thing" is the hard part. As a parent and a helping professional, I have had many moments thinking to myself, *That's nice, but like, how do I actually make that happen?* Or I've read a method someone has provided and thought, *But how does that actually play out in real life?*

The Courage to Communicate Model

Part One: Adult Pre Work

1. Do your research- Get informed
2. Find your people- Seek support
3. Cull the knowledge- Determine what to share
4. Shape your family's beliefs and values

Part Two: CHANGES Tool

5. **The Communicating**
C- Communicate what happened
H- How do you feel/What do you think?
A- And today...
N- Nerves, worries, and fears?
G- Going forward...
E- Everyone and everything that can help
S- Silly and serious questions

Part Two again!

Part Three: Adult Post Work

6. Feel and release
7. Move forward

With the intention of keeping the CTCM grounded in real life, let's consider using the tool with real-life stories, from real-life people, fresh in our minds.

BEN'S EXPERIENCE . . .

My partner and I recently separated after twelve years of marriage. We were fairly amicable with each other and had not been obviously fighting. Thus, we knew that the separation was going to come as a shock to our nine-year-old daughter. We also knew going into it that our daughter is more emotionally attached to her mother, and that transitioning to not being with her full time would be particularly difficult.

Before telling our daughter about the separation, my partner and I spent time coming up with an initial plan of what life would look like after the separation so we could tell her what to expect. When we actually told her, it was hard, and we all had a good cry together. We were careful with how we communicated the change to her, keeping our message as simple and direct as possible while telling her the initial plan. We didn't go into details about why we were separating, as we didn't want to make it too complicated when we first told her. But we made it clear that she could ask any questions she had in that moment or as they came up in the future. We also made sure to tell her repeatedly that it was not her fault whatsoever, that there was nothing that she could have done or could do to change it, and that any emotions that she felt were okay. We also told her that we were still a family, even if how our family was organized was changing, and that we had made this decision because we believed that it would ultimately be best for all of us.

Thankfully, our basement suite was unoccupied, so I was able to move in there initially to help the transition be more gradual. At first, she still slept every night in her familiar room upstairs and we alternated putting her to bed (as had been our routine before). We then moved to one night a week in her new bedroom downstairs and have increased it from there. As much as we could, we gave her control over what she could keep upstairs in her bedroom and what she took downstairs to her new bedroom. We also gave her the opportunity to decorate her new room. Our beautiful daughter has moments of big emotion as she processes this change, and it has been a hard transition for all of us, but we are holding her in love together and slowly finding the new rhythm of life.

Ben is a father, son, partner, co-parent, registered social worker, and professional counselor. Giver of joy-filled smiles and magical laughs, Ben is a gentle friend to many and a thoughtful student of life.

Ben and his partner communicated to their daughter with compassion and love. They also ensured changes happened in her life in increments by shifting her physical situation slowly and gradually. This isn't something that is available to everyone during a life change, but it is a beautiful example of the choices we have in the middle of change and how we can accommodate our children's need for slow transitions. If these parents had wanted to follow a structured communication tool, the CHANGES tool could be an option for them and other caregivers in similar situations.

The second part of the CTCM is a template for having *the* difficult conversations. It is quite simple, and I assure you it doesn't require any specific skills or knowledge to use. It's about facilitating a conversation, a back-and-forth between an adult and child, with the sole purpose of supporting the child. It is an exchange of information. The CHANGES Communication Tool provides a *method* so you can be intentional with your words and your process, while still creating a unique experience for the child you are talking to.

You can work through the CHANGES tool with few words actually spoken, and it can still be a roaring success in terms of how your children perceive the support. Coming to your child, with your own needs in check, with the message that you care about their experience enough to stop everything and be with them, is a profound message. To sincerely tell your child that this is their life and that they are in charge of the storytelling rights, is an incredibly respectful form of communication. If you work through the seven steps with minimal words exchanged, but you connect with your child as if their existence was all that mattered during the interaction, you will have a positive outcome. There is no measurement of success that involves how much your child shares or what emotions are identified, because your child is not going to remember what words are said during this conversation anyway. Your child will only remember how they felt.

I wish I could give you a sentence to say or a question to ask that will, without a doubt, tell your child they are safe, secure, connected, and loved through this difficult time, but the truth is, the words do not matter. **All this time we thought we were here working on how to talk with our kids, but as it turns out, we were actually working on how to be present to our child's experience.** If you don't truly believe that your child is the center of their own story and that everything they feel and think is the core of the plot line, all the words in the world will not make them believe what you are saying.

However, every time a tragedy that makes headlines occurs in our world, I see adults desperate for someone to give them the words to explain it to their children. Psychologists post scripts on social media and write blog posts. Parents cling to the scripts, which are just carefully constructed sentences, as the answer to how to help their children feel safe and secure while the news channels report that civilization as we know it is burning down. I know from this observation that providing you with suggested phrases to use when implementing the CHANGES tool is essential to your perception of support. Please keep in mind that the provided scripts, the words, are helpful to us as adults, but they mean nothing to children without the true and honest belief from adults that they are the most important person in their own lives. You don't need specific words, sentences, or paragraphs to be present for your child, but they sure do help.

As I offer you words that you can use to implement the CHANGES tool, please keep at the forefront of your mind that these words are the tiniest part of the intervention—they are just a conduit for connection. I am just another everyday human, offering you a mode of connection. Words are tools, use them or don't use them, but be sure that if you are not completely present and dedicated to what is happening for your child when you engage in this conversation, your words will fall flat.

C - Communicate What Has Happened

I know you might have noticed a lot of things have been different lately. A big change is happening in our lives (your life, our community, in your family). I want to tell you about it.

Describe the situation as best as you can to your child, using the information prepared in the Pre Work steps.

H - How Do You Feel and What Thoughts Do You Have About What Has Happened?

Sometimes when things change in our lives, we feel new and uncomfortable feelings about the change. Sometimes we have good feelings that make us feel happy, and sometimes we have stormy feelings that make us feel mad. Lots of adults have these feelings too. Our minds get busy trying to make sense of all these new feelings, and we end up with new thoughts swirling around in our heads. That is normal. I want to know everything you have been feeling and thinking about [insert specifics to your situation]. Please tell me all the feelings and thoughts you have had since this change started to happen.

A - And Now

It's important for us all to understand what is happening right now. When [insert type of change] happens, some things can't be like they were before. That's what is happening for other families (other schools, other communities, etc.) that are going through something like this as well. Their lives are changing too.

Today . . . [insert information that affects your child's day-to-day situation]

This week, some things are going to be different. For example . . . [insert more changes you know will be in place for the child in the short term]

For the next month or so . . . [insert changes that will still be the same over the next few weeks]

N - Nerves, Worries, and Fears

New and different experiences can feel scary. Sometimes when [insert your situation] happens, we have a lot of worries about what has happened or what might happen next. When those worries build up in our bodies, we can feel sick. We might get a headache, or a tummy ache, or we can want to cry, or hit, or scream. Big worries like that happen for adults and other children too. It can be helpful to talk about the things that scare us and the worries we have in our bodies. Your worries and fears are important to me, and I want to hear every single one. Let's talk about them.

G - Going Forward

Things are going to continue to be different for the next little while, and I don't know everything that is going to happen. Here's what I know will happen for sure . . . [insert changes you know are coming]

Here are some ideas about what might happen [list possible changes that might occur]. No one knows yet what will happen for sure, so all these things are just "maybes." When change happens like this, we have to wait and see how things will go. Other families who are in a similar situation don't know for sure what is going to happen to them either.

E – Everyone and Everything That Supports You

When something happens that we have lots of new feelings and thoughts about, it can be helpful to have people in our lives that help us feel safe and strong. When scary things change, and we feel nervous or worried, it can help us manage if we have things we can do to make our bodies feel better. When I'm sad or scared, I talk to [insert your support person or group of people], and when my mind starts to list all my worries, I [insert something physical you do when you get anxious to feel better, i.e., go for a walk, take a bath, drink some water, take a nap, etc.]
Tell me who you have in your life to talk to.
Give me some names of people who you feel good with when you are around them.
If you could go to the park with one person, who would it be?
If you could play with one person, who would it be?
If you were feeling scared, who would you call?
If you needed help, who would be there to help you?
What activities do you like to do that make your body and mind feel calm?

S – Silly and Serious Questions

When new and different situations happen in our lives like [insert your specific change], we often have lots of questions about what's happening. Sometimes kids wonder silly things like if they'll still get to eat their favorite meal for dinner, and sometimes they wonder serious things like when they will get to see someone they care about again. Everyone has questions, and all questions are normal. I have questions about some of this too. Let's take turns asking each other questions and see if we can help each other find some answers.

Continue asking and answering until your child runs out of questions to ask or feels satisfied in this conversation. Feel free to give your child permission to ask you future questions anytime or to give them guidance on when you're available to answer more questions. For example, it's okay to say: *Every evening after brushing your teeth and before stories, we're going to have a ten-minute question time* (or a similar period of time during the day that suits your schedule) *for you to ask me any questions that come to your mind during the day.*

If finding words that fit for your message is important, there are a lot of other words out there that are available to use. And although it's not all about the words used, it is yet another both/and situation. Just like being present, being calm, and being prepared, words are a part of the connection, attuning, regulating, and empathizing process. As Brené Brown says, "language is the greatest human portal that we have,"[43] so find some words that feel right for you and your family, that help you to express yourself, and to open the door to your child's expression of their experience.

In the words of another solid soul, my friend Kailee writes:

> Can letting go not feel like giving in, and giving in not mean you are giving up, and giving up not reflect as failure? Is it possible that letting go doesn't mean you are less than you should and could be? Could you be enough not trying so hard to hold on to something, someone, some idea that wasn't naturally meant for you? Maybe the void you feel is just space, and when did

space become the enemy? When did the absence of something become nothing? We don't look at the glade and assume it failed to become a forest. Let go.

Kailee. Momma. Professional. Poet. Human definition of "still waters run deep."

YOUR EXPERIENCE . . .

What action steps can you take today to:

Tell your child one specific thing that has happened in the past resulting in this change _____

_____

Ask your child to share with you one feeling they have about what has happened _____

_____

Share with your child one thing that is happening currently _____

_____

Tell your child one thing that might happen next _____

_____

Ask your child to tell you one worry they have about what might happen next

_____

Exchange a question with your child. Ask them a question you have and prompt them to ask you a question they have _____

_____

KEY POINTS FOR REFLECTION:

- Communicating with children involves many aspects other than choosing what words to use.
- It is more important to be present for a child and committed to a child's emotional experience than it is to know how to say the *right* words.
- Language is one of the ways adults can connect, attune, and regulate to a child.

13. METHODOLOGY AND IMPLEMENTATION III: THE ADULT POST WORK

The final section of the CTCM is the Adult Post Work. There are two steps here that we do for ourselves and for our children. These steps help us acknowledge the hard work we've done, mark the completion of this work, and stay regulated to our child or children while we move forward.

Again, we take a peek at a real-life story, because real life is what this is all about. Here Kathryn talks about her experience of loss and grief.

The Courage to Communicate Model

Part One: Adult Pre Work

1. Do your research- Get informed
2. Find your people- Seek support
3. Cull the knowledge- Determine what to share
4. Shape your family's beliefs and values

Part Two: CHANGES Tool

5. **The Communicating**

C- Communicate what happened

H- How do you feel/What do you think?

A- And today...

N- Nerves, worries, and fears?

G- Going forward...

E- Everyone and everything that can help

S- Silly and serious questions

Part Three: Adult Post Work

6. Feel and release

7. Move forward

 you're here (again)

KATHRYN'S EXPERIENCE . . .

I have almost always felt blessed in my life's journey and know that I have always been blessed to live, work, and play in a healthy, happy family in a middle-class, free, democratic country. I had two amazing children, a phenomenal husband, and the ability to take my family and others on regular mission trips to Mexico, feeling that we can give something back in an unfair world. Not without its challenges, my job as a nurse fit well with my passions, gifts, and talents. I was happy and felt in control of life. My Christian faith tells me that God is in control, not me, but the "charmed life" I lived made it easy to support the illusion that I was indeed in control to a degree.

Until I wasn't.

At the age of sixty, my healthy, active husband died within two weeks of hearing about an undetermined liver disease. My grown children and I sat by his bed in ICU for a week as medical staff desperately tried to keep him alive until a liver transplant became available. It was not to be. We turned off the respirator and supported him in his final journey. At the time, my thirty-three-year-old daughter was battling bowel cancer with chemotherapy. Her journey ended six months later, in the hospital with staff valiantly attempting to control her horrendous pain. I lived in that hospital room with her for the last six weeks of her life. She left a two-year-old son and a husband who had no capacity to cope with any of the events of the past year.

Change. In a way that was, in my wildest dreams, never imagined. My life changed in every way. My son-in-law returned to his home country with my grandson, my son's new marriage didn't survive the traumas of that year, I could no longer manage our hobby farm and sold it and the animals, our dog died—the subject of a bad country song! And in the process, I knew I needed to grieve well to be able to live wholly somewhere in the future.

(Kathryn's story continues later in this chapter.)

STEP 6 - FEEL AND RELEASE

This is the step where we have the opportunity to acknowledge the hard work we just completed and release the built-up energy. Depending on your family culture and what you like to do, your way of releasing energy may be unique to you. Some families plan pizza and movie nights so they can be together and recharge. Other families read stories in forts or paint rocks after collecting smooth pebbles from the beach. If you are the type of family that looks for a physical outlet, take your kids to the swimming pool or the local lake, creek, river, or ocean. Get hot chocolate and go throw rocks into the water. Walk into the woods or dig in your garden. Take your kids to a new park with the biggest slide you can find. Swing on swings until you can't swing anymore.

If it's available to you, just for you, run, hike, ride, do yoga, lift weights.

Make playdough, make mud pies, roll out pizza dough . . . and of course, bake cookies.

Something to note here is that sometimes releasing energy isn't as pretty as art, crafts, and outdoor fun. Sometimes children's bodies release stress, sadness, anger, and upset without the child having any choice about the release. Crying, shaking, and vomiting are all normal ways the body regulates its nervous system when releasing trauma (supporting a child to release stress through their body can be difficult and upsetting, but this type of release is normal and healthy).

This step of the CTCM prompts you to do something for yourself and your child to acknowledge it in whatever way feels best for you. Tell no one, tell everyone. There is no right or wrong way to pause, reflect, feel, release, and then move forward.

EDUCATORS AND THERAPISTS

Something to consider if you are a classroom teacher or office-based professional is that often when children have completed a difficult task or worked through a challenging lesson plan, their reward is a break away . . . from you. They get to head outdoors for recess, hang out with peers over snacks, or go home to play video games. Often, this is when their teachers get a break too. Or when teachers move to a different room to teach a different class. Or when counselors see their next client. If we look at this step as an essential opportunity to share our regulation with our students and clients, then they need to feel and release *with us*. This step becomes part of the lesson as the educator models for their students how acknowledging, celebrating, and releasing looks. Or it becomes part of the work if you are a professional working one-on-one with a child. My suggestion with this step is that part of the work is doing something to feel and release all the energy, emotion, and effort built up during the process of communicating. Activities like baking, cooking, swimming, or bike riding may not be available to you like they are for some parents, but this step asks you to be creative to provide something physical that allows the children you are working with to release. You likely already do a version of it and have a ton of tools in your tool kit. If you are in a small space, some mess-free options are: sensory bins, fidget toys, music and dancing, blowing up balloons, pre-made slime, etc. You get the idea. Think of things you can do with your class or your clients so that if someone walked by your open door they would think, *Oh, there they go playing with slime again while wiggling on wiggle cushions.* What the open-door spectator doesn't realize is that what looks like playing is actually an intentional act to use the body to nurture healthy brains. Literally any time someone suggests or minimizes the opportunities you give the children you work with to release through play, please hold onto the image of their brain, all lit up with multiple pathways zigzagging across the brain's surface like jam-packed highways of information.

STEP 7 - MOVE FORWARD

Our final step offers us an opportunity to show our children the end of our work and how to move forward. Life is a constant evolution, and change will continue to occur, but it is important to acknowledge the completion of this process just as you would the wrap-up of a family meal. Will you have dinner again tomorrow? Yes. And the next night, and the next night, and the next night. Yet we still teach our children to ask to be excused from the table and to bring their plates to the sink, because dinner is done for *this day*. In the case of change, the work is done for *this day*. As you share with your child that the CTCM process is complete, if this type of communication experience is new for your child, likely two things are going to happen:

1) Your child will feel a sense of security, safety, and contentment with their newfound understanding, and you will see a settling. A calming of questions, of intense behaviors, and of anxiety (which can look like a decrease in previous issues like sleep disturbances, wetting issues, nail chewing, clothing chewing, appetite issues, etc.). This settling is healthy. This quietness may appear like your child has gone quietly inward, and that is okay. The tiny human you care about is okay.

Or

2) This new world of information will be so exciting and interesting to your child that they will want to dive deep into knowing All. The. Things. They may be peppering you with all the hard questions, all the time. For them, knowing how things work will be freeing and will create a sense of safety or control in their world, so they will seek more and more and more. Get ready for all the bedtime questions, all the backseat follow-up thoughts while you're driving to the store, all the dots they are connecting in their lives. It may even appear like a fixation on the change or like an explosion of external processing, and that is okay. This rapid processing and interest could look like an increase in intense behaviors, and that's okay too. The tiny human you care about is okay.

As we move forward, we follow our children on their journey and meet their needs by being resourced with the tools to communicate so no conversation is too hard. Nothing our child needs information about is too scary, too shameful, too sad, or too painful to talk about. We have the confidence to lead them through this change, as well as all the changes that occur as we move forward.

EDUCATORS AND THERAPISTS

Early on in my career, I created a program for children who had been brought into the care of the province of British Columbia and placed into foster homes.

They were all in different situations for different reasons, and my colleague and I met with them weekly during our group time and worked through the curriculum we created. I don't remember much about the course content, but I remember those kids' little faces and the child who gave me lice after she rested her head on me during a piggyback ride. I also remember that when shown images of adults' faces during an activity, the majority of children could not name the very-obvious-to-me expressions being shown. My most vivid memory, however, is that during the last group meeting, we had a graduation of sorts. We invited parents, social workers, and foster parents, and all the adults stood face-to-face and created a tunnel for the kids to run through by joining their hands over their heads. I think we may have said a few words about each little person prior to them running through, and then they ran under all those adults who cared about them, through the tunnel of faces looking down on them with pride, and out toward the light. It was a clear moment of celebration and completion. It marked the end of all the work in a very physical way, both for the adults facilitating and the children attending.

I don't have many other professional recollections where completion of difficult emotional work was celebrated and moving forward was acknowledged. I can think of a handful of times when counselors left positions unexpectedly, never returning to their caseloads. The profession of child safety social work has a high turnover, and the constant change in staffing leaves gaps in the services families receive. And sometimes kids disappear too. More than once I've worked with families where a child never returned to see me while I was in the midst of intentional and purposeful work with them. How many times do children just stop coming to school? Stop showing up to their after-school program? Become unavailable to work with you for reasons beyond your control? And the work is just left hanging.

Whenever we have the chance, we need to create celebrations, acknowledgments, and rituals to mark the completion of this type of hard work. Yes, this work can feel like a loop that we must start again, and yes, change is constant and there is no permanent completion. Yet it is our responsibility, whenever possible, to create the tunnel through which our children can run. Let them run toward the light.

There are no medals for this type of work. No one celebrates (usually), or shares photos on social media, or makes a special dinner with cake for dessert. But I promise you, communicating with a child about the changes that are affecting them is one of the best gifts we can give. Communication is worth celebrating.

Kathryn's story didn't end with her grief. Although grief never left her, her life moved forward.

KATHRYN'S EXPERIENCE CONTINUES . . .

Seven years later, I can now say that I have a full, rich life. I bought a new home that suits my stage of life well, I went back to work for a year, then retired. I remarried two years ago to a lovely man who was also widowed, and we are building a new home. I have good friends and a big family again (my husband has four children and seven grandchildren). And I volunteer as a hospice grief support person and support the dying and their families at Hospice House. Grief is ever a companion on my journey, and I have learned to accept that for the most part.

What have I learned about navigating change?

For me, because of my faith, it's about always leaning on Jesus and recognizing his control and wisdom. There are other very important components to my journey as well.

It's been so essential to have good people around me. I was and am blessed with good, deep friendships, and I am still surrounded with them and their support. They walked beside me, offered minimal advice unless I asked for it, and just loved me. And at times, they knew what I needed before I did and just did it. But it matters that you choose people who can be with you in a way that works. I found myself distancing from some friends, as their support didn't work for me.

Professional help can be invaluable and speaks to strength, not weakness. I saw an exceptional prayer counselor for five years: weekly at first, then tapering as we felt I needed less. I still see her occasionally. Her advice and direction were objective and life-giving. I also accessed hospice support and had a grief support person.

Flexibility and priority. I came to realize that "don't sweat the small stuff" is actually the way forward. What's important changed for me: people, self-care, finding joy, and being kind shaped my days.

- Allowing myself to feel. I believe that grief happens with all change, good or bad. But the way through is to allow those difficult, often overwhelming feelings to surface and to talk about them as needed. And to do that, I had to be kind to myself.

- Kindness to myself also looked like not trying to behave in ways that kept others comfortable. I don't like conflict and have always tried to be there in ways that the person in front of me needs. During this process, I had no space for that. I would sometimes try to go to an event or gathering, only to abruptly get up and walk out when I could no longer manage. And I learned that not only was that okay, but it was also necessary.

- Creating a safe space. I was so raw and vulnerable. It was so important to have a place or people that made me feel safe. My home did that most of the time, as it was my sanctuary, and I had four friends who allowed me to feel both safe and vulnerable. I limited contact with others depending on my rawness at the given time.

- Activity. Walking daily kept me grounded, sometimes on my own, sometimes with my people. To this day, my mental health is improved by daily walking/hiking. Other activities that bring joy rather than deplete mental resources encouraged me to re-evaluate all that I do.

- Through it all, and in the darkest days, I hung on to hope. It enabled me to keep moving forward and see that light at the end of the tunnel, albeit a very faint one at times. And it was helpful to be with others who could also point to that hope when it was so difficult to see it.

Kathryn. Wife, mother, grandmother. Retired nurse. Advocate for maternal and child health. Champion of faith.

Kathryn offers ideas about action steps she took: walking, seeking support, creating a safe space, hanging on to hope, leaning on professional support, and prayer. What action steps fit for you?

YOUR EXPERIENCE ...

Practice taking action steps by:

Today I will do _____

to help me feel grounded and to increase positive feelings for myself.

Today I will honor this hard work by _____

Today I will invite my child to celebrate the completion of this process by

KEY POINTS FOR REFLECTION:

- Although rarely recognized for its importance, the work of communicating with children about change deserves to be celebrated and rewarded.
- Genuine, compassionate, and empathetic communication is a labor of love.
- Moving forward is a process. It's important to take breaks to pause and reflect.

OVEN-READY

When the cookies have been not-so-gently shoved in the oven to bake, and my kids have scampered off with tummies full of sugar and butter, and the dog has given up hoping for dough to fly off the beaters right onto the floor at her feet, and the maniacal hum of chaos relents, all that's left is a messy kitchen. The cookies might be baking but cleaning up the mess awaits. Unlike my mother who would promptly begin cleaning, this is usually where I pause in the doing and step over the mess to make a hot coffee or walk out of the kitchen briefly to take in the view in another room of my home (which may or may not be equally as messy). The expression that life is a beautiful mess is true. In my life, it's often a series of beautiful messes that don't necessarily feel beautiful while they are in the making. Change is like that. All the Big Ds have the potential to be awful and ugly and dark and damaging, and then once we're on the other side of the change, we can survey the damage, step away from the mess, and perhaps see the beauty. People often reflect on change as the catalyst for important growth. We hear adults, years later, share their perspective that difficult changes in their lives actually became blessings in disguise. *Years later* is the key concept in that sentence. It takes time as adults to gain perspective and grow stronger and braver, and the same is true for children. I would also suggest that it takes support, emotional work, and empathic communication. We can't expect ourselves or our children to see the positive aspects while in the midst of the chaos of change. We would be lacking compassion and understanding if we went into a life change with any expectation that the people around us would welcome it with gratitude and hope.

Like the perfect cookie, our children are sweet and tender. They deserve for us to do the work that needs to be done so that they have opportunities to build their own resources, and to gather their own strengths, so they can become the next generation of caring adults with the tools needed to be empathic communicators. When the cookie crumbles in their life, or in the lives of someone around them, and we can use the CTCM to show them how to feel and talk through a change, they will carry that skill forward. Although *Crummy Conversations* is about how to talk with children, has it become clear that the basis for communication is being present and attuning to our child's needs? The seven-step model offered in the CTCM gives caring adults a way to create safety and security for children so they can feel and process their emotions, without fixing or managing the child's experience. If the question is: How do we talk with our children about change? The answer is: We show up and *be* for them.

If you've made it here with me, whether you skimmed chapters or read every word, I hope you feel like you have the support you need. I hope you know that there is a way you can support yourself to talk with a child. If you still feel fearful or full of self-doubt about your ability to communicate to your children, that's okay. Sometimes we just have to move forward and try our best because we know how important it is. You may be reading this book because you know how important it is for your child to understand a challenging time in their life, and even though you feel unsure, you will try to support them through it. Using your presence and your words, you will be there for them because you are *courageous*. I have created this model, and I am sharing it with you because I am courageous too. Nobody has it all figured out, and we may stumble over our own limitations, but we will gather the supports, tools, and resources available to us to do the best we can for our children, because we know that they deserve it.

Maybe my perception that I have a trio of skills is actually a quartet of skills? Cookie baking, empathy, communication, *and* courage? Here I am using difficult life experiences like my parents' divorce, my own divorce, my perceived lack of security in childhood, and my continued fear of grief and loss to inform and deepen my desire to be with my children in a soft and vulnerable way. These challenging life changes have given me an opportunity to practice using softness and sweetness to create strength and growth. They have also given me the opportunity to reframe some of my experiences and use them to inform a model that I feel passionate about. Looking at my own life through the lens of the CTCM gave me the nudge I needed to take back the pen on my own life story. And that took real courage. Facing change by looking it straight in the face and talking about it, like you have done, takes real courage too. My belief that baking a mean batch of cookies is a learned skill, just like empathy, communication, and resilience are learned skills, extends to courage as well. We aren't born courageous; we become courageous with practice. When we use the CTCM to walk with our children through a change experience, we are practicing these life skills ourselves while giving our children the opportunities to practice these skills as well. As we come through the other side of change by implementing the CTCM, we have:

- Used empathic communication to show our children that their experience matters to us;
- Shown them that they are secure, safe, and connected to a caring adult;
- Modeled our strength and courage in being vulnerable, honest, and open;
- Created an opportunity for them to practice their own sweet and soft strength;
- Demonstrated that we believe they are the stars of their own stories and that they get to hold the pen to their histories;
- Been present for them when they needed us and used our BE-ing as the solution to a challenging life experience; and
- Increased their potential for resilience and decreased their exposure to compounding trauma by literally growing their brains through our attunement to their needs. We have co-regulated with them so beautifully by completing the CTCM that we have grown their neural pathways. In real life.

And while their brains have been supported and nurtured to grow, building new pathways and creating new snappy connections, our adult brains have grown too. As we worked through the CTCM, we have inadvertently looked at our own experiences and unintentionally nurtured and supported our own adult brains through this process as well. Even if that was never our intention, it will have occurred to some degree. In helping our children, we have helped ourselves. By being present, loving, caring adults for our children, we have been loving, caring adults for the child that still lives inside of us. Just as creating this model and bringing it forward into the world is a portion of my personal evolution, it may be a portion of your evolution as well. What may have at first seemed like *just* a model to help children through change may have, in fact, been a model to help adults through change too.

Could it be possible that in my attempt to create a model that contributes to the prevention of emotional hardship experienced by children that I am actually offering a resource for children and adults to move through change *together*? Is it less about adults taking action to support children to heal and more about adults and children healing together? In our attempt to walk our children through their feelings, have we walked ourselves through our feelings too? Back in the bookstore, latte in hand, am I walking the rows and rows of books now looking for a hybrid section? **Is it possible that the solution we needed wasn't a parenting book focused on children or a self-help book focused on adults, but a *feeling* book focused on the human experience?**

Maybe.

Regardless, as we pause in the mess, stand in the metaphorical kitchen, and hold off on cleaning up, let's stand in the glow of our courageous communication. Let's breathe in the safety and security we created for ourselves and our children. Let's close the book on this chapter of our lives but keep the pen in our hands for all the chapters coming after this one.

And then let's eat the cookies.

COOKIES, FOR REAL

We can't wrap this up without including an actual cookie recipe. I also can't include a recipe without also including a few hot tips from an unprofessional cookie baker.

COURAGE TO COMMUNICATE COOKIES

AN ACTUAL COOKIE RECIPE | FOR EVERYBODY

ingredients

- 1 cup salted butter (soft-ish)
- 1 cup brown sugar
- 1 cup white sugar
- 2 large eggs
- 2 teaspoons vanilla extract
- 2.5 cups all-purpose flour
- 1 teaspoon salt
- 1 teaspoon baking soda (dissolved in 2 teaspoons hot water)
- 3/4 cup dark chocolate chunks or chips
- 3/4 cup milk chocolate chunks or chips
- Flaky sea salt (optional)

directions

1. Cream together the butter and sugars in a stand mixer for a bit.
2. Add the eggs and vanilla- scrape down the sides of the mixing. bowl as needed.
3. Add the salt, baking soda/water slurry, and flour. Mix on low until everything is looking like cookie dough.
4. Stir in the chocolate chunks or chips.
5. Drop by ice cream scoop-fulls onto a lined cookie sheet.
6. Bake at 350 degrees for 10-12 min.
7. Bang or drop the pan on the counter or stove top when you first take the cookies out of the oven. Sprinkle tops with sea salt.
8. Let cool 5 min before removing from cookie sheet.

Cookie tips!

- Always use salted butter, plus add additional salt.
- If mixing with a mixer-type machine, use the flat beaters instead of the round whipping beaters (the flat beater is better for creaming the butter and sugars without adding air).
- Fun trick: run your cold brick of wrapped butter under hot water for a few seconds and then push on one end. The butter will magically slide right out of its tight little wrapper.
- It is not the end of the world if you have to soften your butter in the microwave because you forgot to take it out of the fridge.
- Cut-up chocolate bars, chocolate wafers, or chocolate chunks make extra delicious chocolate "chip" cookies.
- Ignore what the recipe tells you about baking time. Ovens are different, and a timer will fail you. Remove the cookies from the oven when the cookies have golden edges and soft centers. If in doubt, under bake.
- I always drop my cookie pans with intention onto the top of the stove when I take them out of the oven. Alternatively, you can open the oven door about halfway through baking and give the tray a little lift and drop. It's called pan banging, and it helps your cookies have beautiful little ripples around the edges.
- Replace some of the flour in a recipe for pulverized quick cooking oats (just blend in your blender or food processor). You'll get a delicious dough with a little more chew.
- In most recipes, including the one above, you can swap out the chocolate chips for coconut, chopped pecans, smarties, raisins, or any similar item you have on hand.

Most importantly, cookie recipes are like people: there are lots of different kinds, and you just have to find one you like.

ARE YOU A TOUGH COOKIE?

This book is for all the other tough cookies out there. We are the people who want to remain sweet and soft while being brave enough to do the hard work required to be healthy and present adults for the children around us. It requires a lot of emotional muscle to do hard things while remaining vulnerable. Talking to our children about painful life changes from an open, curious, and compassionate place takes a lot of courage. We know that if we are guarded, defensive, and judgmental that we are feeling fearful and insecure, and that's not the type of *cookies* we want to be. Our type of toughness knows that every time we have a courageous conversation, we grow stronger. We show our children that facing our hard days with honesty and compassion is how we move forward. Tough cookies, like us, communicate to children in a way that shows them softness and sweetness *is* strength. Be a tough cookie with me and show the children in your life the type of tough cookie they can be too.

ACKNOWLEDGMENTS

There were so many points in the writing process of this book when I wished my content was a little more like a hilarious Samantha Irby essay and a little less like a deep dive into the inner workings of my heart and soul. During those moments, I leaned heavily on my close-knit circle of cheerleaders, believers, and trusted confidants. For every Sunday morning hike when my beloved friends asked for writing updates and encouraged me to keep going—thank you. For every moment of self-doubt that my mom washed away with words of wisdom and comforting reassurance—thank you. For every day of frustration and struggle that my husband walked me through with logic, patience, and tolerance—thank you. For the times I needed to bounce ideas and check my thinking and my brother and sister-in-law where there with solid answers to my murky questions—thank you. For everyone in my corner who read early drafts, suggested changes, celebrated the little wins along the way, inspired my stories, shared an encouraging word, and believed in my ideas when I didn't believe in them myself—thank you.

To the colleagues, families, and children who have shared their stories, their strength, and their struggles with me—thank you for entrusting me with your teachings.

To those who contributed their stories and shared their voices to bring my model to life—thank you for your generosity and your leap of faith in this project.

To the professional helpers, who paved a path to healing for me by holding space, treating me with the utmost respect, and for giving me the gift of change by believing in my own capacity for growth and expansion before I did—thank you.

To the YGTMedia publishing team, Sabrina Greer, and the Author Generator Society community who gave me permission to be a writer and to share the full expression of who I am, without titles, labels, or credentials—thank you.

To my babies, who did not afford me the time or space to write at my leisure and instead made me sneak in writing sessions in the early morning hours, after bedtime, and in between playdough, bike rides, and nonstop snack prepping—thank you for keeping me grounded in what matters most. I love you.

Lastly, thank you to baking cookies and throwing pots, both of which have taught me with every batch of burned cookies left in the oven too long and every clay bowl cracked in the bisque kiln that we might as well enjoy the process, because life is rarely about the outcome.

And man, was the process of writing this book *sweet.*

WORKS CITED

1. Brackett, Marc. *Permission to Feel: Unlocking the Power of Emotions to Help Our Kids, Ourselves, and Our Society Thrive*. Celadon Books, 2019.

2. Dr. Vanessa Lapointe. Instagram. https://www.instagram.com/dr.vanessalapointe

3. Lapointe, Instagram.

4. Canadian Institute for Health Information. "Children and Youth Mental Health in Canada." https://www.cihi.ca/en/children-and-youth-mental-health-in-canada

5. CNN Health. August 10, 2021. Sarah Molano. "Youth depression and anxiety doubled during the pandemic, new analysis finds." https://www.cnn.com/2021/08/10/health/covid-child-teen-depression-anxiety-wellness/index.html

6. Brackett, Marc. *Permission to Feel: Unlocking the Power of Emotions to Help Our Kids, Ourselves, and Our Society Thrive.* Celadon Books, 2019.

7. Carrington, Jody. *Kids These Days: A Game Plan for (Re)Connecting with Those We Teach, Lead and Love.* Impress, 2020.

8. Canadian Centre for Addictions. September 3, 2019. Lisa Linnel-Olsen. "Addiction Among Youth: What Is Happening in Canadian Classrooms." https://canadiancentreforaddictions.org/addiction-youth-canadian-classrooms/

9. The National Benefit Authority. February 5, 2015. Akiva Medjuck. "Canadian Teenagers Struggle with Eating Disorders." https://www.thenba.ca/disability-blog/canadian-teenagers-struggle-eating-disorders/

10. missingkids.ca. https://missingkids.ca/en/resources/runaway/

11. The High Court. October 12, 2021. Elma Mrkonjić. "20 Heartbreaking Missing Children Statistics [2021 Update]." https://thehighcourt.co/missing-children-statistics/

12. Canadian Centre for Child Protection. July 27, 2021. "New Statistics Canada crime data shows victimization of children intensified during pandemic." https://protectchildren.ca/en/press-and-media/news-releases/2021/stats-canada-crime-data-pandemic

13. Tanis Frame. https://tanisframe.com/play-evangelist/

14. Divine Conversations. March 9, 2020. "Ep. 3 - Parenting 2.0: A New Paradigm Shift in Parenting with Dr. Vanessa Lapointe & David Loyst." https://www.himalaya.com/episode/ep-3-parenting-2-0-a-new-paradigm-shift-in-parenting-with-dr-vanessa-lapointe-david-loyst-divine-conversations

15. Wilcox, Leisse. *Alone: The Truth and Beauty of Belonging*. YGT-Media Co., 2021.

16. Wiest, Brianna. *When You're Ready, This Is How You Heal*. Thought Catalog Books, 2022.

17. Jacqueline Neligan. Verbal. Permission to use.

18. Carrington, Jody. *Kids These Days: A Game Plan for (Re)Connecting with Those We Teach, Lead and Love*. Impress, 2020.

19. Smith, Will and Mark Manson. *Will*. Penguin, 2021.

20. White, Michael and David Epston. *Narrative Means to Therapeutic Ends*. WW Norton, 1990.

21. VeryWellMind. July 14, 2021. Jodi Clarke. "What Is Narrative Therapy?" https://www.verywellmind.com/narrative-therapy-4172956

22. Brackett, Marc. *Permission to Feel: Unlocking the Power of Emotions to Help Our Kids, Ourselves, and Our Society Thrive*. Celadon Books, 2019.

23. Faber, Adele and Elaine Mazlish. *How to Talk So Kids Will Listen and Listen So Kids Will Talk*. Scriber, 2012.

24. Faber and Mazlish. *How to Talk So Kids Will Listen and Listen So Kids Will Talk*.

25. Author's words, not direct quotes from resource.

26. Author's words, not direct quotes from resource.

27. Faber, Adele and Elaine Mazlish. *How to Talk So Kids Will Listen and Listen So Kids Will Talk*. Scriber, 2012.

28. Based on Dr. Vanessa Lapointe's work in *Discipline without Damage* (LifeTree Media, 2016) and *Parenting Right from the Start* (LifeTree Media, 2019).

29. Siegel, Daniel J. and Tina Payne Bryson. *The Whole-Brain Child: 12 Revolutionary Strategies to Nurture Your Child's Developing Mind*. Bantam, 2012.

30. Maté, Gabor. *The Wisdom of Trauma*. Documentary. https://thewisdomoftrauma.com/

31. Based on Gabor Maté's work.

32. Maté, Gabor. *The Wisdom of Trauma*. Documentary. https://thewisdomoftrauma.com/

33. Based on the work of Brenda Lucas. BC Association of Clinical Counsellors. https://bcacc.ca/counsellors/brenda-lucas/

34. Center on the Developing Child – Harvard University. "ACEs and Toxic Stress: Frequently Asked Questions." https://developingchild.harvard.edu/resources/aces-and-toxic-stress-frequently-asked-questions/

35. Edward Tronick, Bruce Perry, Megan Gunnar, and Daniel Siegel have all studied and written about it.

36. VeryWellMind. July 28, 2021. Kendra Cherry. "The 6 Changes of Behavior Change: The Transtheoretical or Stages of Change Model." https://www.verywellmind.com/the-stages-of-change-2794868

37. Aha! Parenting. Laura Markham. "The Surprise Side Benefit of Regulating Your Own Emotions." https://www.ahaparenting.com/read/Change-Your-Child

38. Carrington, Jody. *Kids These Days: A Game Plan for (Re)Connecting with Those We Teach, Lead and Love.* Impress, 2020.

39. Carrington, *Kids These Days: A Game Plan for (Re)Connecting with Those We Teach, Lead and Love.*

40. A note for clarity: neurotypical means most typical (normal), neurodivergent means not typical (not normal), and neurodiverse refers to a group of people who represent both (think neurodiversity, like biodiversity).

41. https://drvanessalapointe.com/

42. Lapointe, Vanessa. *Discipline without Damage: How to Get Your Kids to Behave Without Messing Them Up*. LifeTree Media, 2016.

43. Facebook. June 2, 2022. "Brené Brown. Atlas of the Heart – Official Trailer." HBO Max.

YGTMedia Co. is a blended boutique publishing house for mission-driven humans. We help seasoned and emerging authors "birth their brain babies" through a supportive and collaborative approach. Specializing in narrative nonfiction and adult and children's empowerment books, we believe that words can change the world, and we intend to do so one book at a time.

 www.ygtmedia.co/publishing
 @ygtmedia.co
 @ygtmedia.co

Made in the USA
Las Vegas, NV
11 October 2022

57024291R00131